Twelve Apostolic Women

TWELVE APOSTOLIC WOMEN
Joanne Turpin

ST. ANTHONY MESSENGER PRESS
Cincinnati, Ohio

Scripture citations are taken from *New Revised Standard Version Bible,* copyright ©1989 by the Division of Christian Education of the National Council of the Churches of Christ in the U.S.A., and used by permission. All rights reserved.

Cover and book design by Mark Sullivan

Library of Congress Cataloging-in-Publication Data

Turpin, Joanne.
  Twelve apostolic women / Joanne Turpin.
    p. cm.
  ISBN 0-86716-525-1 (alk. paper)
  1. Women in the Bible. 2. Bible. N.T. Gospel—Criticism, interpretation, etc. 3. Bible. N.T. Acts—Criticism, interpretation, etc. I. Title.

  BS2545.W65T87 2004
  225.9'22'082-dc22

                         2003025701

01 02 03 04 05 06 07 10 9 8 7 6 5 4 3 2 1

CONTENTS

For today's Apostolic Women
especially Greta Burden and Victoria Ries

INTRODUCTION

More Spirited Than Lions

"Buried treasure" is a popular way of describing stories about women in the New Testament. For rarely, if ever, are they included in books about saints presented to us as role models, let alone find their way into homilies as women to emulate. Choices for Sunday readings do little to highlight their contributions. Nevertheless, it is not too much to say that their dedication to Jesus and to the spread of his message after his death helped lay the foundation of Christianity.

To begin with, Jesus' most loyal disciples proved to be the women who had served him during his Galilean ministry, and remained faithful to him even when authorities in Jerusalem sentenced him to death as a political criminal. (The male disciples had gone into hiding.) Historian Michael Grant observed that "this superiority of the women's behavior was so embarrassing to the Church that its writers would have omitted it had it not been irremovable… setting the seal on the exceptionally close relations they had enjoyed with Jesus throughout his ministry…" (*Jesus*, p. 85).

That they did not waver in their fidelity to the cause was made clear when a man named Saul, in an effort to stamp out the Jesus movement, considered women important enough to "the Way" that he arrested them as well as men. After his dramatic conversion, now as the apostle Paul, he came to rely on women's help.

One needs to understand how much their lives changed once Jesus willingly accepted them as his disciples. Theirs was a society that believed, in the blunt words of Josephus, a first-century Jewish historian: ". . .says the Scripture, 'A woman is inferior to her husband in all things.' Let her, therefore, be obedient to him; not so that he should abuse her, but that she may acknowledge her duty to her husband; for God hath given the authority to the husband" (*Against Apion,* II, 25). In varying degrees, this belief underlaid the thinking of other societies in provinces throughout the Roman Empire, not just in Palestine.

When "the Way" began to spread across the empire, women often played a pivotal role in the establishment of house churches, the basic institution of the infant church. Both Acts and Paul's letters give testimony to that.

Referring back to the New Testament era, Church Father John Chrysostom (A.D. 347–407), in a commentary on Paul's Letter to the Romans, wrote: "For an honor we have, in that there are such women among us, but we are put to shame, in that we men are left so far behind by them. . . . For the women of those days were more spirited than lions" (quoted in *Biblical Affirmations of Woman* by Leonard Swidler, p. 295). Chrysostom's comments are all the more noteworthy because he generally viewed women in negative terms.

New Testament women could be considered apostolic in the way they lived and labored, carrying out the mission Jesus entrusted to his disciples and to all who would follow later: preaching the Good News through word and deed. Few are their recorded words in Scripture, though actions undeniably speak volumes. But what we do hear are words that resound through the centuries, as they voice some of Christianity's most profound beliefs. Martha of Bethany, for one, professes a faith in Jesus virtually identical to Peter's confession of faith. And Mary of Magdala is the first to proclaim news of the Resurrection to the male disciples. "I have seen the Lord!" she exclaims. (They refuse to believe her.)

All of the women portrayed on these pages are known to us from the New Testament: in the Gospels, Acts of the Apostles or Paul's letters to various Christian communities. Incidentally, Acts in its original Greek title, *Praxeis Apostolon*, is literally rendered "Some Acts of Some Apostles." In Greek grammar, when the definite article is omitted, the adjective "some" is understood.

While New Testament passages serve as the primary source for the stories that follow, other, non-biblical, sources of information help to develop a more complete picture of the lives of these apostolic women.

To begin with, there are Christian writings from the early centuries (history, commentaries and other kinds of literature) that extend our knowledge of their world, and in some cases make direct reference to them.

In our own time, biblical scholarship and archaeological finds add to the store of knowledge, helping to set the stories in context. For it is important to see the women in relation to their place within society, in both the public and private spheres: the social expectations and restrictions, cultural environment and historical circumstances in which they nevertheless spread Jesus' message of Good News. Often it meant overriding the boundaries ordered by society for their gender.

Traditions also play a part in putting some finishing touches on the portraits drawn by the New Testament. It must be noted that not all traditions can be accepted at face value, however. On occasion, they may be the result of pious imagination rather than based on reality. A classic example: the second-century apocryphal gospel that gives details of Mary's childhood, including the names of her parents as Joachim and Anne. Though lacking either scriptural or historical substantiation, this type of "information" is intended to satisfy the natural curiosity people feel in wanting to know the object of their devotion more personally.

Certain tales labeled as tradition are truly fanciful; for instance, the legend originating in medieval times that relates how Lazarus, Martha and Mary of Magdala sailed to Gaul after expulsion from their native Palestine. (The legend gave a boost to the popularity of pilgrimage shrines in southern France dreamed up for the faithful.)

Traditions used in this work are, for the most part, generally accepted as having a basis in fact. They can often be traced to treasured remembrances from a very early date, handed down orally from one generation to the next before eventually being committed to writing. For example, because Christians continued to live in Jerusalem over the years, that ongoing witness enabled Queen Helena, while on a mission to the Holy Land in A.D. 326, to identify sacred sites of the first century—those hallowed by memory.

By weaving together the various strands of information extracted from Scripture passages, history and sociocultural practices of the first century, along with traditions long held dear, a narrative emerges in which we get a much closer look at the women in our stories.

It may be recalled, by the way, that Luke, in his writings, shows how Christianity moved out from Palestine to other provinces of the Roman Empire, and finally to Rome itself, the heart of the empire. Borrowing from the best, we begin our account with women who became disciples of Jesus in Galilee, going on to Jerusalem, spreading the Word to the Mediterranean coast and beyond—Asia Minor and Europe, before reaching Rome.

Although that world of two millennia ago may, on the surface, appear markedly different from our own century, in another sense important parallels can be found. Now, as then, we are experiencing unsettling times. Now, as then, we are called to respond to society's needs and those of our own family and faith community. Now, as then, we long to have our spiritual hunger satisfied and lead meaningful lives.

The twelve women portrayed here speak to us across the centuries, for they embody the enduring values and virtues necessary in answering the needs and longings of every age. Values and virtues are gender-free, so that what can be learned from these models of apostolic living is applicable to men as well as to women.

The stories teach us much about discipleship, about the diverse ways in which it might be incorporated into our own lives. For these women dealt with questions of discernment, commitment, moral courage and loving service—to name just a few.

These are subjects explored further in the faith-sharing suggestions for discussion that follow each story. While the material is designed first of all for group discussion, the individual reader too may find fruit for reflection and, ultimately, decision-making.

In the prayer that concludes each chapter, we first address the woman profiled concerning what she has to teach us about her particular kind of discipleship; and then we seek divine guidance in strengthening our resolve, so that we too can make ready to follow the Way of the Lord.

CHAPTER ONE

Peter's Wife,
Missionary and Martyr

She must have felt some concern when Peter went off with his brother Andrew and several other young men to join the throngs that were gathering at a fording place along the Jordan River. They wanted to hear a fiery preacher called John the Baptist, who attracted disciples as well as crowds. Impulsive her husband might be, but surely not...

Concern changed to anxiety when they returned home to Capernaum and made a shocking announcement: the men intended to give up fishing in order to do more exciting work, though not as followers of the Baptist but, rather, of a Galilean named Jesus. This, on top of her mother's worsening illness, was almost too much to bear.

Surely one of the most overlooked women of the New Testament, Peter's wife is never identified by name. (Customarily, women were identified by their relationship to a man.) One of Paul's letters, however, and early Christian history make reference to her. More about that later.

In the Gospels, she is known only by inference. Jesus, in one of his first miracles, cures her mother of a raging fever—malaria the likely cause. A preview of what lay ahead for the family became evident that same evening, which Jesus spent with them. Once news circulated through Capernaum, the whole town, it appeared, arrived on their front doorstep, many in the crowd seeking healing. (Perhaps the children slipped out to tell neighbors that grandmother was miraculously well again. Tradition, by the way, gives the name Petronilla for a daughter of Peter.)

> "...Peter left his wife at home when he became a disciple of Jesus (Mark 1:22; 10:28). Later, however, Peter's wife accompanied him in his travels outside Palestine (1 Corinthians 9:5)."
>
> —Paul Barnett, *Jesus & the Rise of Early Christianity: A History of New Testament Times* (Downers Grove, Ill: InterVarsity Press, 1999), p. 232.

Life would never return to normal again for Peter and his wife, as their home in Capernaum quickly became headquarters for Jesus' ministry in Galilee.

At this point it may be helpful to visualize the setting, considerably aided by the findings of Franciscan archaeologists. Excavations show that three or four houses would be grouped around a central courtyard shared by all the families. Black basalt, abundant in the area, was the common building material. Roofs consisted of mud thatch and branches.

During this stage of her life, Peter's wife served as a stay-at-home disciple, providing indispensable hospitality for Jesus and his countless visitors, in addition to her many duties as wife and mother. When Jesus was "at home," as the Gospels refer to the times he is in residence, her obligations multiplied. There was, for instance, table fellowship, that hallmark of Jesus' ministry, in which meals had to be prepared for members of Jesus' company. They included even "sinners" like Matthew, once a despised tax collector. Peter would remember him well from the days Matthew extracted customs duties every time Peter took his extra catch from Capernaum to the fish-processing factory in Magdala. He and his wife must have wrestled with the fact that because breaking bread together was virtually religious in nature, then "sinners"—that is, social outcasts—ought not to participate. But Jesus saw things differently.

Perhaps just as unimaginable for a fisherman's wife, company might turn up in the form of distinguished doctors of the Law, religious authorities from as far away as Jerusalem. They came to Capernaum to investigate, and challenge, Jesus' teachings as well as his deeds, even the miraculous ones.

One memorable healing in that situation occurred on a day the house was filled to overflowing, spilling out into the courtyard and even into the street. Friends of a paralytic, carrying him on a pallet, were unable to get through the crush of people, and so proceeded up the outside stairway. Tearing a hole in the roof wide enough to let the man through, his friends lowered him down on his pallet to Jesus' feet. When Jesus forgave the paralytic's sins before telling him to rise to his feet, scribes sitting opposite Jesus ignored the consequent miracle, instead finding fault with the forgiveness aspect. But crowds in those days were still on Jesus' side, and Peter's wife needed to concern herself only with the practical matter of repairs to the damaged roof.

"About 400 the pilgrim Egeria wrote: 'At Capharnaum the house of the Prince of the Apostles has become a Church: the walls of the house are still preserved.' "

—Eugene Hoade, O.F.M., *Guide to the Holy Land* (Jerusalem: Franciscan Printing Press, 1974), p. 918.

Other incidents that occurred specifically in "the house" appear most often in Mark's Gospel, traditionally believed to be based on remembrances of Peter. His wife's role in preparation of meals and attendant daily chores in making Jesus' life as comfortable as possible was hardly the stuff of drama, thus unremarked upon. This was the period thought of as the happiest of Jesus' ministry. Reflecting upon it in later years, she could take satisfaction in that.

In the future, she could also be grateful for the treasured times when Jesus gave private instruction to the inner circle of disciples gathered in her home. As will be seen, when she became a "fellow minister" with Peter, it was important for her to be well-grounded in Jesus' teachings. Perhaps she accompanied the band of disciples when they journeyed to Jerusalem for pilgrimage festivals. But even from a distance, based on what her husband told her, she would know of the mounting opposition to Jesus in the religious capital, eventually to culminate in the horrific crucifixion, to be followed, incredulously, by the Resurrection.

During Jesus' lifetime, Peter had emerged as spokesman for the Twelve, and now he became the logical leader of the Jesus movement, bent on perpetuating "the Way of the Lord." His wife would remain supportive by maintaining the Capernaum household. From archaeological work, it can be assumed that "the house" was the appointed gathering place for believers in Galilee, and for disciples returning for visits home to Galilee. (Of the original Twelve, all but Judas of Iscariot were natives of the province.)

In spreading the faith, Peter, often accompanied by the apostle John (of the Zebedee family), began evangelizing first in Samaria and in urban centers along the Mediterranean coast of Palestine. Peter was also known to travel three hundred miles north to Antioch. During this period, having been in Jerusalem for a Passover festival, he was targeted by authorities for his activities and imprisoned, though it was miraculously of brief duration. Dread must have filled his wife's heart when she heard the initial news, followed by overwhelming relief when he rejoined the others.

As time wore on, the idyllic harmony of believers noted in Acts began giving way to differences of opinion over the admission of Gentiles to the movement, a situation leading to the historic Council of Jerusalem (circa A.D. 50). Once the problem was resolved through compromise, Peter drops from sight as far as Acts of the Apostles is concerned. Acts turns its attention now to Paul. (Luke, the author of Acts as well as the Gospel bearing his name, accompanied Paul on some of his missionary journeys.)

At an unspecified stage, Peter's wife began traveling with him. Their children would have been grown, though the couple was still relatively young. (Girls typically married by about the age of fourteen; boys, usually a few years later.) Their missionary work can be gleaned from early church traditions, the rare historical mention, and observations made in Paul's letters that were preserved in the New Testament.

The first direct reference to Peter's wife (though she remains unnamed) occurs in 1 Corinthians 9:5, a letter written in the mid-50s, in which Paul notes that the apostles' wives travel with them, singling out Peter as an example.

There were definite advantages in having a female coworker, as Paul himself discovered. A Jewish man was free to address a synagogue congregation—often the first stop abroad for a Jew, even a Jewish Christian one. But for him to give private religious instruction to a woman, Jew or Gentile, would give rise to scandal. Only another woman had access to women's quarters. Peter's wife would, of course, be well-grounded in Jesus' teachings, having heard them firsthand.

The extent of the couple's travels is suggested by 1 Peter, a pastoral letter of encouragement to fledgling Christian communities in five provinces of Asia Minor (modern Turkey). Elsewhere, Paul remarks on Peter's influence with the community in Corinth (on mainland Greece).

Eventually the couple reached Rome. The year and circumstances are subject to conjecture, though traditions offer some possibilities. What is known is that they were present during the persecution of Christians in Rome, A.D. 64–67, by the Emperor Nero.

The story of the martyrdom of Peter and his wife is found in the pages of *The History of the Church,* written by Eusebius, a bishop in the Holy Land during the first decades of the 300s. In it he quotes from a much earlier source, *Miscellanies (Book VII),* written by Clement of Alexandria (circa A.D. 150–215). This work describes how Peter's wife suffered martyrdom just before him:

> We are told that when blessed Peter saw his wife led away to death, he was glad that her call had come and that she was returning home, and spoke to her in the most encouraging and comforting way, addressing her by name: "My dear, remember the Lord." Such was the marriage of the blessed, and their consummate feeling towards their dearest.

Afterword

The house that became Jesus' home during his Galilean ministry is today a shrine. That astonishing fact is owed to the diligent work of Franciscan archaeologists in the Holy Land.

Though pilgrims in the early Christian centuries gave witness to the fact that the house in Capernaum was used as a center of worship, what later happened to it was a mystery. Until, that is, the 1960s when funding became available for excavations at a site by the Sea of Galilee, and Capernaum, lost to the world for centuries, was unearthed. Franciscans at first focused on reconstructing the ruins of what turned out to be a fourth-century synagogue. Their labors went on to include the area neighboring the synagogue. In the process, the ruins of a fifth-century basilica came to light. Digging deeper, archaeologists uncovered a first-century house beneath the basilica. Further investigation revealed that the house had been converted to congregational use midway through the first century, with additional embellishments and enlargements made in succeeding centuries. The accumulated evidence points to this being the house of Peter and his wife, making it the oldest Christian sanctuary still in existence.

Faith-Sharing Topics

When her home became the base for Jesus' ministry, Peter's wife found her life turned upside down. But as a faith-filled woman, she met the challenge. When unforeseen events cause stress or upheaval in our personal world, we can draw strength from an inner peace that remains despite storms that swirl around us.

> *What spiritual disciplines might contribute to your inner peace?*
>
> *Where or how do you find the coping skills to meet new challenges?*
>
> *Not all unforeseen events are unhappy ones. When was the last time the God of surprises surprised you?*

Peter's wife made the transition from a stay-at-home disciple to missionary work abroad. The in-between years allowed her time to prepare for a new vocation. Looking ahead to the next stage of life, we can simply let it happen or plan for the future, thereby smoothing the way.

> *When have you experienced a significant transition, and how did you deal with it? How resistant were you to change?*
>
> *How can structure in our life help us to get through a difficult in-between period before entering new territory?*
>
> *In discerning what God wants of you, to whom do you go for guidance?*

Prayer

Beloved wife of Peter,
How blessed you were when Jesus crossed
    your threshold,
Though his presence turned your life upside down.
Did you resist the change?
Were you beset at first by worry and fear?
Those are my feelings in uncertain times.
Yet you became a disciple, serving the Lord.
Could you ever have imagined what lay in store
When you made a home for Jesus?
Lord Jesus,
Help me to make room in my heart for you,
So that when sudden change comes into my life,
I will feel the strength of your presence.
When anxieties plague me
Over circumstances beyond my control,
Let my trust in you increase,
For faith in you
Will unfailingly sustain me.

CHAPTER TWO

Salome, Wife of Zebedee

One can almost hear Zebedee exclaim, "Not only my sons, but now my wife, too!" He would well remember the day when, barely recovered from the shock of his sons James and John declaring that they were leaving the family fishing business in Capernaum to become disciples of an itinerant preacher, his wife Salome announced her intention to do the same. Bad enough to lose the help of James and John, though he already employed extra workers and could always hire more. But the services of a wife were not so easily replaced.

A woman's labor was no small matter. A host of daily chores awaited her attention. Much of the work was carried out in the central courtyard shared with several other families. Fortunately, the subtropical climate by the Sea of Galilee allowed for outdoor living much of the year. In cooking from scratch, first came the grinding of grain for the dietary staple— bread, baked in the communal oven that stood in the courtyard. While the children played, their mothers cooked soups and stews of legumes and vegetables over a portable stove, moved indoors during inclement weather. Meat was costly, therefore eaten only on special occasions; but fish was plentiful in the region of the lake. Women grew vegetables in nearby plots, and also tended small livestock. These included chickens, kept chiefly for the eggs; goats, which supplied milk and byproducts of curds and cheese; and sheep, raised mainly for their wool. Cloth was spun from looms set up outdoors. At harvest time, field labor might be necessary, though in fishermen's families, wives were more likely to help mend nets and sails.

> "...[I]t appears that one could confidently say that Jesus of Nazareth opened a new era in the history of women."
> —Francis J. Moloney, S.D.B., *Woman: First Among the Faithful* (Notre Dame, Ind.: Ave Maria Press, 1986), p. 32.

Salome's original motivation in becoming a follower may have stemmed partially from a wish to keep an eye on her sons as well as attend to their practical needs. The young men's temperaments were of such a nature that Jesus had dubbed James and John "Sons of Thunder." (On one occasion, they had asked Jesus to make use of his wonder-working ability and call down fire from heaven on some Samaritans who proved less than hospitable.)

The Gospels do not mention Zebedee attempting to dissuade Salome from her decision. But perhaps her own nature was such that there would be no point in opposing her.

In the beginning, when prospects for the success of Jesus' mission held such promise, Salome, like all the disciples, must have reveled in being a part of the undertaking. For her, there would be an added attraction: the opportunity to exercise talents beyond managing a household, however worthy that might be.

Both social attitudes and religious regulations legislated against women exercising a public role of any kind in the community. Salome's breaking out from the traditional pattern surely caused talk, though perhaps she sought to lessen it by claiming the protection of her sons.

In Jewish society, the stepping-stone to power of any kind lay in knowledge of religious law, even if one wished to serve in lesser capacities, such as the town council or local court. Females, however, were denied the necessary education to do any of that.

While boys attended synagogue school, where they were instructed in the law, girls received their schooling at home from their mothers in order to learn how to look after a home and understand their religious duties. This meant, primarily, observing dietary regulations in the preparation of meals, and keeping ritual purity laws. The latter emphasized regulations surrounding menstruation, which had as their effect a monthly curtailing of social life as well as participation in community worship.

In the long-ago, as Salome would have learned from listening to biblical readings at the synagogue or the recounting of beloved tales during religious festivals, at least a few women had played prominent roles in the history of her people. Stories were told of heroic deeds and even of women in positions of authority. Miriam, for instance, saved the life of her baby brother Moses, in defiance of a mighty Pharaoh's order that all male Jewish babies be killed.

> "There is every evidence that this mother [Salome] and her sons and their father Zebedee gave of their substance as well as of themselves all during Jesus' ministry. The mother was one of that faithful band of women whose special sympathetic service helped His mission."
>
> —Edith Deen, *All the Women of the Bible* (New York: HarperSanFrancisco, 1983), p. 194.

Deborah had been a "judge," a title reserved in the past for leaders who arose out of a need for someone qualified to dispense justice or command armies. Deborah's bravery in battle was legendary. Compilation of the Bible in written form owed its start to the prophetess Huldah, who was consulted when a scroll was found in the Temple. Hers was the authoritative voice that authenticated it as a sacred writing.

But by Salome's time, restrictions on women's activities abounded, coming in reaction to the secular, foreign influences that threatened to blur Jewish identity. It was left to women to uphold the honor of their society. Being above reproach, acting in accord with standards set by men, was their paramount obligation.

Yet now here was Salome, once dutiful wife and mother, going about the towns and villages of her province as part of a traveling band of a charismatic preacher. Though holy men of personal magnetism were something of a tradition in Galilee, the religious establishment in Jerusalem viewed them with suspicion; for *Hasidim,* as holy men were called, acted too independently, even in their practices of piety (often outdoing the establishment). Some received financial support from women who, of course, never dreamed of accompanying these men in their work.

How frequently or how far Salome traveled with Jesus' band is unclear; though in several Gospel passages we find her either somewhere on the road or in Jerusalem. Getting around Galilee was facilitated by the many roads that criss-crossed the province. Among the major ones, the *Via Maris* ("Way of the Sea") was an ancient trade route carrying considerable traffic from the Nile Delta to Damascus, Syria. From the Mediterranean coast, it cut across Galilee, to head up the west side of the lake, passing towns such as Magdala and Capernaum. Other highways had been built to provide ease of movement for the Roman military, though everyone made use of them: merchants, government officials, royalty, farmers taking produce to market and travelers in general.

Galilee was thickly populated. Some scholars estimate the population at about 365,000. Josephus, who briefly governed the province in the 60s, wrote of there being 204 towns and villages.

Jesus' excursions, as seen in the Gospels, took him at times west to the border with coastal Tyre and Sidon (in modern

Lebanon), and east of the lake to the far side of the Jordan River. Sometimes he went south to Jerusalem by way of Samaria.

When going on foot, people averaged fifteen to twenty miles a day. It is possible that, for most of the time, Salome accompanied Jesus' band to the towns and villages within a day's journey from Capernaum. The Plain of Gennesaret, scene of a number of Jesus' activities, was just a mile and a half south of Capernaum. After a day spent helping with the crowds, Salome could easily have returned home by nightfall—no doubt to the delight of Zebedee.

Although Galilee was rich in agriculture, towns rimming the western side of the thirteen-mile-long lake were also bustling urban centers from which Jesus could draw sizeable crowds. Mark describes a typical scene: "And wherever he went, into villages or cities or farms, they laid the sick in the marketplaces, and begged him that they might touch even the fringe of his cloak; and all who touched it were healed" (6:56).

Women could be of particular use when crowds like this converged on Jesus. While the ailing on cots and litters waited their turn for Jesus' healing words and touch, the skills women acquired in tending the sick in their own homes could be transferred to the larger stage. A reassuring word to relieve anxiety, a drink of water, whatever else was necessary to make the person more comfortable.

When crowds gathered to hear Jesus preach in the countryside, away from town or village, different needs could arise, as happened in the one miracle reported by all four Gospels. With the day wearing on, and no one prepared to leave, feeding the people became the problem. A major one, for the multitude numbered some 5,000 men—"besides women and children," adds Matthew.

When Jesus directs his disciples to organize everyone into groups of fifty it is easy to picture the female disciples rounding up the children who had strayed from a mother's side, or helping older folks and the handicapped get settled on the grass. After a young lad volunteers his five loaves and two fish for starters, Jesus miraculously multiples the offering so that all in the crowd are fed. In the end, twelve wicker baskets full were left over. It has been suggested that the baskets originated with women in the crowd who typically are never without carriers of some sort if they have small children in tow.

In John's Gospel, the miraculous feeding prompted the people to try and crown Jesus their king. That may still have been on the minds of his followers as they journeyed south to Jerusalem. On the way, an incident occurred that "the mother of the sons of Zebedee" was not likely to forget. Both Matthew and Mark tell the story.

In Mark's account, James and John ask Jesus that they be given the most prominent seats—to the right and left of Jesus—in the coming kingdom. The two, after all, had been picked, along with Peter, as part of the inner circle of male disciples. In Matthew's version, their mother makes the request. Jesus replies not to her, however, but turns instantly to her sons, admonishing them that they have failed to understand what he has been talking about all this time. In both Gospels, Jesus stresses the importance of their taking up the cross. (Salome had her job cut out for her: making amends for her sons' unseemly ambition.)

As Jesus hung on the cross, Salome would be present to show support in the face of a hostile mob. She is also named among the women who went to the tomb on Easter morning.

Afterword

It is probable that, after the Resurrection, Salome returned home to Zebedee, and to Capernaum, where help was needed to build up the faith in the province. Though Acts tells virtually nothing about this phase of the Jesus movement, Salome surely became an active part of the house church belonging to her neighbors, Peter and his wife.

Acts gives an account of her son James' death. He was the first of Jesus' twelve to suffer martyrdom, beheaded during Passover, circa A.D. 44, on orders of Herod Agrippa I, who served briefly as king of Judea. As one of Jesus' inner circle, James would have been a natural target. He is sometimes referred to as James the Great. Salome's son John was the only one of the apostles who apparently did not become a martyr, but ended his long life in Ephesus, where tradition says he wrote the Gospel of John.

Faith-Sharing Topics

In Salome's world, women knew exactly what was expected of them as wives and mothers. (Men knew their place, too.) Crossing boundaries invited criticism, contempt, and even exclusion from society. In American society, the freedom to choose one's way of life has probably never been greater, but family expectations or the limitations we place on ourselves can negate that freedom.

> *When have you aspired to do something out of the ordinary, then told yourself "no" because...*

> *God has a plan for your life. Can you see how unique it is?*

> *In making lifetime choices, the following steps should be considered...*

Once Salome made her commitment, she remained steadfast in her undertaking, from Galilee to the tomb. Today's society is characterized by a general reluctance on the part of individuals to make long-term commitments, most notably in regard to relationships and work.

> *What do you judge to be some of the impediments to making a commitment?*

Has your world been personally affected by lack of commitment on someone's part?

Do you foresee a change in attitude any time soon? What would bring it about?

Prayer

Faithful Salome,
You heard the words, "Follow me,"
And you took them to heart.
Words of the cross did not dissuade you,
But there were words of promise too,
And moments of pure joy.
Oh, the sights you beheld:
Miracles of healing,
Miracles of love.
Lord Jesus,
We, too, want to follow in your footsteps.
Teach us to walk in your ways.
Though our steps may falter at times,
Know that we desire nothing but to please you,
To do God's will.
Strengthen our resolve so that,
Like Salome, we may remain steadily on the right path,
True to the end.

CHAPTER THREE

Mary, Wife of Cleopas

Villagers of Nazareth, incensed by Jesus' words spoken to them in the synagogue, attempted to throw him off the brow of a cliff above the village (see Luke 4:28–30).

Later, when Jesus moved the base of his ministry to the more receptive atmosphere of Capernaum, some of his kinsmen went there with the intention of seizing him, declaring that he must be mad. They regarded Jesus' activities as an embarrassment to the family, and wanted to stop him. However, the crush of people around Jesus that day made it impossible for them to carry out their plan.

Despite opposition from within the ranks of his own relatives, Jesus could count on support from one branch of the family—the one headed by Cleopas. (A second-century church historian identified him as the brother of Joseph.) It may be remembered that Cleopas, with another disciple, encountered Jesus on the road to Emmaus after the Resurrection.

In the Gospels, the name of Mary, wife of Cleopas, appears more often than his. She is described as having been a follower during the Galilean ministry, and was also among the women present at the crucifixion and the tomb in Jerusalem.

Mary and her husband were parents of one of the twelve apostles, James the Less, as distinguished from Salome's and Zebedee's son, James the Great. Though the latter was the better-known of the two, in Jesus' egalitarian ministry, "the Less" more likely indicated a shorter stature or a younger age. In the Gospels, James the Less is further identified as the son of Alphaeus, which is the Roman (Latin) equivalent of Cleopas. It was not uncommon for Jews to bear both a Roman and a Hebrew or Aramaic name. (Aramaic was then the spoken language in Palestine.)

> "Its [Galilee's] people provided him with his first disciples, and its dense scattering of settlements formed their first mission field."
>
> —John J. Bimson, consulting ed., *Baker Encyclopedia of Bible Places* (Downers Grove, Ill.: InterVarsity Press, 1995), p. 138.

The Holy Family and that of Cleopas and Mary had a close and enduring relationship, as judged from a scene in John's Gospel, where the two Marys stand alongside each other at the foot of the cross—bound in love as well as familial ties.

It can well be imagined that during the time of grief, followed by the glorious Resurrection, the two sisters-in-law shared many memories of their sons growing from infancy to adulthood in the village of Nazareth. (Extended families traditionally lived in proximity to each other.)

Nazareth is situated in a basin in the highlands, fifteen miles southwest of the Sea of Galilee, and twenty miles from the Mediterranean Sea. During the first century, in an estimated population of five hundred, there were farmers, shepherds and a handful of craftsmen, such as Joseph the carpenter. Life was typical of agricultural villages. Though people worked long hours, they found enjoyment in family and community celebrations, such as the wedding in nearby Cana. At harvest time in Nazareth, all the villagers took part in treading grapes for the production of wine.

Despite the bucolic setting, Nazareth was not remote from the wider world. The term "backwater" sometimes applied to it does not do justice to the geographical facts. About six miles to the south of Nazareth, the Via Maris, a major international highway, crossed the Plain of Esdraelon. And within walking distance, some three and a half miles to the northwest, lay Sepphoris, capital of the province during Jesus' boyhood. The population of Sepphoris, estimated at forty to fifty thousand, rivaled that of Jerusalem. For Gentiles as well as Jews living in the capital, it provided the amenities of any cosmopolitan city. Its marketplace served the needs of surrounding towns and villages.

> "Women were clearly counted as among those who were taught by and who traveled with Jesus as 'disciples'....These women broke with Jewish custom in order to leave their homes and travel openly with Jesus."
>
> —Barbara J. MacHaffie, *Her Story: Women in Christian Tradition* (Minneapolis: Fortress Press, 1986), p. 15.

About two years after Jesus' birth, Herod the Great died. During the brief power vacuum that followed, uprisings broke out across the country, from north to south. When Galilean rebels seized an arsenal at the fortress-palace in Sepphoris, the Roman army moved in, retaliating by wreaking devastation upon the city and crucifying any rebels they captured. Crosses bearing the bodies lined the roads.

When order was restored, one of Herod's sons, Antipas by name, inherited Galilee as his princedom, and he set about rebuilding Sepphoris. Upon the Holy Family's return from refuge in Egypt, Joseph may have found employment during the city's reconstruction period, which lasted until circa A.D. 10. (Carpenters worked in building construction in addition to crafting household furnishings and farm implements.)

In the meantime, Jesus would have begun attending synagogue school along with his male cousins. Mary and Cleopas had six children: four sons, named in Mark 6:3 and Matthew 13:54–58. (The two daughters remained nameless.) After school hours, a boy also began learning a trade by working alongside his father. At age fifteen, formal apprenticeship began.

Luke's Gospel relates the single incident known about Jesus' boyhood, in which the family went on pilgrimage to Jerusalem. (It is believed to be based on remembrances of Jesus' mother.) Youths approaching the age of thirteen were encouraged to take part in a pilgrimage to the Temple. The occasion was meant to instill in them the rights and responsibilities entailed in becoming "sons of the covenant." For at age thirteen, males were accepted as full members of their faith. (The ceremonial bar mitzvah was a later development.)

Although three pilgrimage feasts were celebrated each year, the spring festival of Passover held the greatest spiritual significance. Every town and village made up a caravan for all who could afford taking the time to travel to the holy city. Going by caravan ensured safety, for brigandage on the roads constituted an ever-present danger. Depending on the route taken, the journey from Galilee, close to a hundred miles south, could take anywhere from four to six days each way. The festival itself lasted a week.

Men and boys usually traveled in one part of the caravan, women and girls in another. Whether the Cleopas family took part in this particular journey, they would be well-acquainted with what occurred after the feast had concluded.

In the confusion of packing up and starting home to Nazareth, Joseph and Mary each apparently thought that Jesus had accompanied the other one. Not until the end of the first day did the parents discover their son was missing. Anxiously they hastened back to the city, while the rest of the caravan waited for their return. Eventually Joseph and Mary found Jesus in the Temple, conversing in a manner beyond his years with the renowned doctors of the Law who taught in the precincts of the sanctuary.

Did Jesus' mother ever tell her sister-in-law about Jesus' mystifying words then, and what they might have meant? Is that when Mary of Cleopas first became aware that there was something unique about her nephew? There are so many unanswered questions about this period of Jesus' life. Luke's Gospel notes only that, after the Temple episode, Jesus remained dutiful to his parents.

At an undocumented time, Joseph died, and Jesus apparently took over his father's workshop and the care of his mother. And so life went on, until the day Jesus told his mother about a higher call. He must have made arrangements for someone in the family to assume his responsibilities, perhaps one of his cousins. In any case, after Jesus announced his intention, his Aunt Mary, not long afterward, made her own decision. For she is identified in all four Gospels as being part of Jesus' company during the Galilean ministry. (She may also have served as the eyes and ears for Jesus' mother.)

Not until late in Luke does the reader learn that Mary's husband had also become a disciple at some point. Cleopas could have been among the unnamed seventy (Luke 10:1) sent ahead on one occasion to prepare people for a visit by Jesus. He was clearly present at Jesus' last Passover pilgrimage to Jerusalem. For in one of the most commented-on scenes of Jesus' post-Resurrection appearances, Cleopas and a companion depart Jerusalem, disheartened by the tragic turn of events. On the road they meet the Risen Lord, but fail to recognize him until, stopping at an inn for a meal, they recognize him in the breaking of the bread. And then Jesus vanishes. They rush back to the city to tell the others.

Cleopas' wife Mary may have remained in Jerusalem to give comfort to her grieving sister-in-law. In any event, all of the followers of Jesus were gathered in an upstairs room when

Cleopas and the other disciple burst in to tell their astonishing news.

Matthew's Gospel reports Mary's own encounter with the Risen Lord (28:1-10), which also occurred along a road, but in Jerusalem. It has never received the attention given that of her husband's. Perhaps because she recognized Jesus immediately, and there's no story in that?

Afterword

The Cleopas family could rightly be called a holy family, too. On the calendar of saints are Mary, James and Symeon. James (the Less) is mentioned once in the beginning of Acts, along with the other apostles. Tradition has him preaching in Persia, where he was martyred.

Cleopas' unnamed companion on the road to Emmaus is often guessed at as young Symeon, another son, although Mary's name also sometimes comes up. (In New Testament Greek, a reference to "they" is just as ambiguous regarding gender as it is in English.) Symeon would rise to prominence in the church when he was elected unanimously by the Christians of Jerusalem as the second overseer, or "bishop," of their community. The first head, after Peter and John left to become full-time missionaries, had been the James who is referred to as "brother of the Lord" (or possibly cousin). This James was martyred by stoning in A.D. 62, on orders of the high priest.

With the disastrous war against Rome approaching, Symeon led his flock to refuge in Pella, on the other side of the Jordan River, for the duration of the war. Later, during a persecution by the Roman Emperor Trajan (ruling circa A.D. 98-117), he was crucified.

Historical records indicate that descendants of Jesus' kinfolk continued living in the area around Nazareth until as late as the third century.

Faith-Sharing Topics

Mary recognized a holiness in Jesus that many others in Nazareth failed to see. It led to her becoming one of his disciples. We can easily miss what is before our eyes when we look with preconceived notions.

> *How would you define holiness? What are its chief characteristics?*

> *Have there been times when you failed to recognize the extraordinary in what at first glance seemed ordinary?*

> *Can you suggest ways in which to call forth the gifts of others and to encourage their development?*

Mary and Cleopas were successful in passing on religious values to their children. They knew how to nurture faith. Anyone who deals with youngsters—teachers, godparents, counselors—has opportunities for nurturing faith. But the family home is the ideal starting point.

> *"Family time" means ...*

> *Can you see a spiritual underpinning to having regular family meals—breaking bread together?*

> *What has your family, or any you know of, done to create rituals at home, making it sacred space? Describe them.*

Prayer

Wise Mary,
What stories you could tell!
Of a little boy in Nazareth
Growing up to be pure goodness, pure holiness.
Somehow you saw in him
What others were too blind to see:
That Jesus is the Answer
To all the world's woes,
All the world's longings.
Lord Jesus,
Grant me the vision
I so often lack:
To recognize the best in others,
To see each person I meet today
As a child of God,
Worthy of God's love.
This I resolve,
For your glory and the good of all.

CHAPTER FOUR

Joanna, Wife of Chuza

One of Jesus' most loyal disciples—a woman named Joanna—came from the royal court of Herod Antipas. Her social prominence was owed to the high position her husband, Chuza, held in Antipas' administration. Chuza served as steward, or finance minister, managing the vast royal estates—agricultural land that netted much of Galilee's wealth. Because of Chuza's close working relationship with the tetrarch (Antipas's princely title), it is reasonable to assume that Joanna was privy to much that went on behind the scenes.

The capital for the province was now Tiberias, a new city Antipas had built along the shores of the lake. The palace itself, home for the court, occupied a site on a hill above the lake. The government bureaucracy included both Jews and Gentiles. The city, too, consisted of a mixed population, for whom a Hellenistic lifestyle prevailed. "Hellenistic" refers to a way of living in which Greek customs and language were adopted. Though Rome wielded the power, Greek culture had won out in the admiration department, and was copied throughout the empire, particularly in major urban centers. Tiberias could boast of the typical entertainment facilities of any Greco-Roman city, including theatre, hippodrome and public baths. In deference to his Jewish subjects elsewhere in the province, those observant in religious practices, Antipas made a show of keeping the important holy days.

As to palace life, historians and archaeologists give evidence that every material comfort could be had. Amid luxurious surroundings, its occupants enjoyed the most delicious foods and finest wines as their daily fare. (Court society also fed on gossip, talk of fashion and the excitement of intrigue.) In dress, courtiers wore the best in linens, silks or fine woolen. Hours might be spent by a servant or slave arranging a woman's elaborate hairstyle in preparation for a banquet.

The Tiberias palace was just one of those Joanna would have been familiar with. For when the tetrarch traveled, his retinue was expected to accompany him. Among the palaces that members of the Herod family made use of, major ones included those at Jerusalem, Jericho (their winter resort) and Machaerus, the fortress-palace east of the Dead Sea.

> "Since there is no reason to think that Chuza joined her on this journey, one must imagine that either a very tolerant husband is in view or that, more likely, Joanna has left him—purse, dowry, or inheritance in hand—to follow Jesus."
>
> —Carol Meyers, general ed., *Women in Scripture: A Dictionary of Named and Unnamed Women in the Hebrew Bible, the Apocryphal/Deuterocanonical Books and the New Testament* (Boston: Houghton Mifflin, 2000), p. 103.

Machaerus is remembered for being the scene of John the Baptist's execution. As the Gospels relate, it happened at an infamous banquet, when Herodias, wife of Antipas, schemed to bring about the Baptist's beheading. The fiery preacher had earlier been imprisoned at Machaerus after his public denouncement of the affair between the royal couple, calling it both adulterous and incestuous. Now Herodias had her revenge.

One can speculate that the ugly episode precipitated Joanna's decision to leave the court. Known for certain is that she met Jesus (Luke's Gospel does not give the circumstances), and he healed her of a serious illness—a meeting that changed her life.

Any crisis of ill health can give rise to a reexamination of one's life, of one's priorities. Joanna could not fail to contrast the self-indulgence and pettiness of court society with the generosity of spirit and camaraderie she witnessed among Jesus' company of disciples. In any event, subsequent to her miraculous recovery, she astounded the court with her announcement that she was leaving that privileged life in order to travel about the land in a very different kind of society, led by an itinerant preacher. (Not that Jesus was an unknown figure; by this time, Antipas had expressed the desire to see the wonder-worker face to face.)

> "No man seems to have taken the risk that she [Joanna] took in Jerusalem, a member of the court identifying herself with a traitor to the state."
>
> —Elisabeth Moltmann-Wendel, *The Women Around Jesus* (New York: Crossroad, 1987), p. 139.

Nothing is mentioned of Chuza's reaction. He may have objected strongly, to no avail. (Joanna's future activities would show her to be a person of courage and determination.) On the other hand, her husband might have initially felt so grateful for his wife's return to health that he decided to humor her for the moment, thinking she would come to her senses once the novelty of this new adventure wore off.

As regards Antipas, Joanna must have realized that the displeasure (or possibly amusement) of the tetrarch could swiftly turn to vengefulness when he realized she had no intention of returning. Nor would she be a conduit of inside information about Jesus, as Antipas might have hoped. Joanna may have had still more to fear from the demonstrated vindictiveness of Herodias. According to historians, Antipas lived under her thumb.

There could be no question about what to expect from others in the court. Now Joanna would become the subject of their wagging tongues, their scorn. Where once she journeyed in style, by carriage, Joanna could expect to walk the dusty roads of Galilee, and make the long trek to Jerusalem on foot. Food and shelter would depend upon hospitality wherever it might be offered, even in the humblest abode. Although Joanna had financial resources of her own (noted by Luke), she put her funds at the disposal of Jesus' ministry.

As the disciples made their circuit of the towns and villages of Galilee, Joanna would be well aware that Antipas employed spies, looking for any hint of opposition to his rule. Surely some were present when, on the occasion of Jesus' miraculous feeding of the multitude, people sought to make him king, though Jesus slipped away before that could happen (see John 6:15). Interestingly, a few verses later, John's Gospel reports boats coming from the capital of Tiberias to where the miracle had occurred.

Antipas may have been alerted by Jesus' mysterious talk of a new kind of kingdom, nowhere better expressed than in the beatitudes, in which secular values were turned upside down. For the poor, the beatitudes gave hope. To those in power, it threatened all that they represented.

At times, Jesus spoke in parables. Two that Joanna must have listened to with special attention concerned stewards: in one parable, the steward was conscientious; in the other, he was unjust. One can't help wondering if Jesus glanced in her direction as he began to speak.

In her new associations, Joanna met women from various walks of life, many whose experiences were totally unlike anything she had ever known. There must have been occasions when they talked long into the night.

Joanna's determination probably underwent its most serious test when she dared to enter Jerusalem with Jesus and the others on what we call Palm Sunday. Their dramatic entrance could not be ignored by the authorities. Among them was Herod Antipas, in the city for the Passover festival. None of the annual pilgrimage feasts to the Temple carried more overtones of nationalism, or more religious fervor, than did Passover. And with that tinderbox combination, insurrection always remained a possibility.

Jesus had chosen his moment of declaration. In mounting a donkey, rather than a horse, to ride down the slope of the Mount of Olives, he enacted the messianic prophecy of Zechariah, coming as a humble emissary of peace, not a political figure. (Warrior kings rode horses.)

Pilgrims crowding the Mount of Olives—many of them Galileans—spread their cloaks on the ground ahead of Jesus, in the manner of greeting royalty, and cried out, "Blessed is the king who comes in the name of the Lord!" After such a public demonstration, trouble was inevitable.

After the arrest, when Pilate learned that Jesus was a Galilean, he sent him to Antipas for interrogation. But Jesus refused to answer any questions; in fact, he uttered not a word. In exasperation, Antipas turned the prisoner over to his soldiers for their amusement; and after that, sent Jesus back to Pilate.

Luke's Gospel is the only one to relate the meeting with Antipas. Joanna has been suggested as the source for that. There is also a tradition that Joanna provided the seamless linen garment worn by Jesus—valuable enough that soldiers assigned to the crucifixion cast lots for it.

Joanna is last seen in Luke's Gospel at the tomb, along with some other women. They are met by two angels, who tell them that Jesus was raised from the dead. "Now it was Mary Magdalene, Joanna, Mary the mother of James, and the other women with them who told this to the apostles. But these words seemed to them an idle tale, and they did not believe them" (24:10-11).

Afterword

In Acts 13:1, we learn that another former member of the court, Manaen, who was also a boyhood friend of Antipas, had become one of the leaders in the church at Antioch (circa A.D. 40). Whether Joanna might have had a hand in his conversion is not known.

Did she return to Chuza? But that would mean returning to the palace—unthinkable for Joanna now. She may have stayed on in Jerusalem, like so many others did, to help with the growth of the movement there.

Her discipleship was still remembered when the theologian Tertullian (circa A.D. 150–225), in quoting from a second-century source, wrote in *Adv. Mare.* 19, 1: "The fact that there were rich women attached to Christ, who also provided for him out of their goods, among whom was the wife of the king's procurator . . ." (As well as a title for governor of a lesser province, a procurator might also be the Roman equivalent of a finance minister.)

Faith-Sharing Topics

Joanna left a more-than-comfortable life in pursuit of a greater good. Detachment—letting go—can involve attitudes as well as material possessions.

> *If you wanted to simplify your lifestyle, what are some of the choices you would need to make? How difficult might you find that?*

> *Would a simpler lifestyle give you more freedom in the way you spend your time? To what benefit?*

> *Can you identify what truly possesses your heart?*

Joanna took a principled stand in both action and words. With that came risk. Making moral decisions in a secular world can require courage as well as wisdom.

Recall a time when you felt compelled to take an unpopular stand. Was there a personal cost?

How has your faith supported your decision-making?

Have there been occasions in which you remained silent rather than upset people? Then wished afterward that you had spoken up?

Prayer

Courageous Joanna,
Without a look back,
You abandoned a kingdom
Founded on selfishness and domination.
Instead you chose selflessly
To serve the Prince of Peace,
Despite risk to your name, perhaps to your life,
As the powers of darkness
Waited their chance.
Lord Jesus,
In the Gospels you assure us,
Time after time:
"Take courage! It is I. Fear not."
Help us to remember your words.
Deliver us from our fears.
Give us the courage
When our conscience tells us,
To speak now! Act now!

CHAPTER FIVE

Martha and Mary of Bethany

Whenever Jesus journeyed to Jerusalem for one of the pilgrimage feasts, he could count on a place to stay, even though lodgings were in short supply at those times. The welcome mat was always out at the home of friends in Bethany, a village less than two miles from the holy city, scarcely a half-hour walk to the Temple.

Bethany lay on the opposite, lower slope of the Mount of Olives, away from the constant din and ceaseless movement of Jerusalem, attributable to its fame as an international city as well as the heart of Judaism. Jesus would appreciate the tranquility of the village after his usual long day of teaching in the Temple porticoes. He would also treasure the hours spent with some of his most cherished friends: Martha, Mary and Lazarus.

Martha is assumed to be the eldest since, in introducing the sisters, Luke says that Martha welcomed Jesus to *her* house. The passage (10:38–42) denotes that a close relationship between Jesus and the family already existed, in this clearly non-traditional household. Even so, in the absence of their brother Lazarus, it was unthinkable in Jewish society for a male friend to spend time alone with any women in the privacy of their home.

A second shocker is in store. For Mary sits at Jesus' feet, totally absorbed in his words. As would be obvious to any onlooker, Mary's posture shows that she has taken on the role of a student. The first step in becoming the disciple of a sage, or rabbi, was to study his teachings, not from books, but by listening to his words. Females, however, did not do such things unless, in rare instances, the teacher was her father or husband. Whether Jesus invited Mary to become his student, or she concluded that, based on his uniquely egalitarian attitude toward women, she was free to take the initiative, it appears now to be an accomplished fact.

> "Here, in Bethany Christ knew true intimacy and friendship. In a word, the great wonder for which the village is forever famous is itself presented in the Gospels as an act of love."
> —Albert Storme (translated by Gerard Bushell, O.F.M.), *Bethany* (Jerusalem: Franciscan Printing Press, 1973), p. 7.

When Martha complains to Jesus that Mary is failing to do her share of the work in preparing the meal, one suspects there is more to it than that. As the older one, Martha is expected to guide her sister in right ways of conduct. And social convention, along with religious restrictions, weighed against Mary's present behavior. More so, in that the closer to the religious capital one lived, the stricter the rules were for women.

Jesus' response to Martha's complaint indicates he understands what she is really saying, and could be interpreted as telling her that what Mary has chosen could also be Martha's choice. Judging from a later conversation Martha has with Jesus (reported in John's Gospel), she too has taken the opportunity to become a learner.

Family members were to play memorable roles later in Jesus' life. These incidents are prefaced by John's account of

Jesus' arrival for Tabernacles, one of the most joyous feasts of the year on the Jewish calendar. The week-long celebration, also known as the Festival of Booths, was timed to occur at the end of the fall harvest in late September or early October. Its name was derived from the practice of setting up small shelters in fields and vineyards in order to monitor the harvest (and guard against thieves). As part of the festivities, it had become customary for people across the land to construct leafy bowers in their own gardens, on balconies or rooftops. Giving the custom religious significance, it commemorated the forty years of desert wandering after the Exodus, when Israelites lived in tents. Thanksgiving for the harvest also played a part in the observance.

Tabernacles was a pilgrimage festival, drawing pilgrims from throughout the country and also from abroad. Sages were among their numbers, eager to promote their religious perspective through their teachings. They were guaranteed a wide audience in a receptive mood on such a festive occasion.

It was at this Tabernacles feast that Jesus began what was to be his most prolonged period of teaching in the porticoes, those covered arcades on the perimeter of the Temple complex.

> "In John, Mary and Martha are crucial characters. Martha is depicted as the representative of faith and full christological confession. Mary by her initiative represents the active practice of discipleship."
>
> —Bonnie Thurston, *Women in the New Testament: Questions and Commentary* (New York: Crossroad, 1998), p. 89.

Three months later, at the Feast of Dedication (Hanukkah) in December, John shows Jesus still coming daily to preach, not having returned to Galilee. This is the only Temple-centered celebration not biblically mandated as a pilgrimage feast. Rather, it commemorated the rededication of the sanctuary after a victorious struggle (164 B.C.) for religious freedom. The lighting of lampstands in the Temple represented the light of liberty. Jesus' reference to himself being the light of the world would not have sat well with the authorities, who grew increasingly more hostile toward his teachings. During this unsettling period, Jesus would find even more comfort in the peaceful evenings with his Bethany friends.

A failed attempt was made to arrest him during the feast, followed by a threat to stone him. Jesus wisely retreated to comparative safety on the other side of the Jordan, where he continued to instruct his disciples.

Early in the spring, the family faced a crisis: Lazarus had become dangerously ill. The sisters sent a message to Jesus about their brother's condition. In careful wording, Martha and Mary left it up to Jesus whether he should risk coming back to the Jerusalem area, but they were understandably hopeful. After all, as John's Gospel describes the relationship: "...Jesus loved Martha and her sister and Lazarus" (11:5).

Mystifyingly, Jesus postpones his return until four days after the burial of Lazarus has taken place. Told of his approach up the road from Jericho, Martha runs out to meet him, while Mary remains at the house with those who had come to mourn with the family. According to custom, in the first week of grieving, family members ordinarily left the house only to visit the tomb.

For Martha to stand out on the road, speaking with a rabbi in public, violated social mores. But she has much to say to Jesus. Unhappiness over his delay registers in her voice: "Lord, if you had been here, my brother would not have died" (John 11:21).

Jesus did not have to tell Martha what she already knew: that in popular belief, the spirit left the body after the fourth day. Under these circumstances, the miracle about to happen could not be questioned later.

In the conversation that ensues comes a moment of revelation from each side. Jesus declares that he is "the resurrection and the life. Those who believe in me, even though they die, will live, and everyone who lives and believes in me will never die" (John 11:25-26). He asks Martha if she believes him.

Her affirmation is immediate, despite her beloved brother's being still cold in the grave. "Yes, Lord, I believe that you are the Messiah, the Son of God, the one coming into the world" (John 11:27). Her faith in Jesus is expressed almost word for word when compared to Peter's confession of faith, though under far different circumstances. Martha's proclamation will, however, take second place to the stupendous miracle that occurs moments later, when Jesus calls Lazarus forth from the tomb. (It is the first appearance of Lazarus in the Gospel.)

News traveled swiftly to members of the religious establishment in Jerusalem. Some may actually have been among the mourners. The family's upper-class status can be deduced from the fact that the tomb of Lazarus was of the elaborate kind, cut from rock, and affordable only for the wealthy.

Miracle or not, authorities were more concerned about the possibility of the populace getting out of hand in their mounting excitement over the miraculous event. To maintain control of the situation was paramount. And so plotting against Jesus began in earnest.

Once again he withdrew from the area, though only to Ephraim, hardly more than a dozen miles to the north of Jerusalem. His stay was short, for he had every intention of attending the upcoming Passover.

Six days prior to the feast, Jesus is back in Bethany, at a banquet held in Simon the Leper's house to honor his return from Ephraim, and to celebrate Lazarus' return from the grave. While Lazarus reclines at table, in banquet fashion, with Jesus and the other guests, and Martha is busy serving, Mary enters the dining room. It is her turn to observe the rules of hospitality, though with a special touch of her own.

She may have heard stories about another occasion, when Jesus was a dinner guest at the home of Simon the Pharisee (see Luke 7:36–50). Simon had neglected the duties of a host in almost every way: not seeing that Jesus' feet were washed as was customary upon a guest's arrival; not giving a welcome kiss; not anointing his head as a sign of refreshment.

There will be no shirking of duty here. In her hands Mary carries an alabaster jar filled with priceless spikenard—an ointment equivalent in value to a worker's wages for a year. She breaks the jar to release its entire contents, profusely anointing Jesus' feet. She then unbinds her hair to wipe up the excess. (A woman would never unbind her hair in the presence of men.)

When the men in attendance gasp at the liberality of Mary's act (wastefulness, some call it), Jesus defends her, saying she has performed a prophetic act, in preparation for his burial. (Feet of the deceased were ordinarily anointed.) He praises her for her beautiful deed, one always to be remembered, and admonishes the men, reminding them of what he has been teaching throughout his ministry: service done with love is what matters most. He will reinforce that teaching days later, when he washes the feet of the disciples.

Afterword

In the Gospels, Lazarus always remains a shadowy figure, despite being the recipient of Jesus' greatest miracle. That miracle led to the tomb in Bethany becoming the object of pilgrims' attention from earliest days, continuing to the present. From tradition, we learn that the final resting place for Lazarus is believed to be on the island of Cyprus, where he ministered as both missionary and bishop.

As for Martha and Mary, a renowned theologian named Origen (A.D. 185–254) introduced the concept that Mary represented the contemplative life, while Martha modeled the less-spiritual active life. Origen's assessment has been widely endorsed by other commentators ever since.

It can be justifiably argued, however, that their portrayal in Luke and John, taken together, shows them as far too complex to be given a one-dimensional label. Martha has obviously been occupied with more than pots and pans, for she gives voice to a Christological statement not to be outdone in the Gospels. As for Mary, her revolutionary behavior in both Luke and John speaks for itself.

Although the two are almost invariably paired, in one respect the sisters part company. It is in the matter of feast days. On the calendar of the Western Church, Martha is accorded a feast day (July 29), but Mary is nowhere to be found. Regrettably, back in the fourth century, Scripture scholars became confused over the number of Marys in Jesus' life, and were further confounded by several anointings performed by women—some named and others anonymous.

The Eastern Orthodox church never lost sight of Mary of Bethany's beautiful deed, and remembers her on its calendar of saints.

Faith-Sharing Topics

Martha and Mary were blessed to spend many hours in the company of Jesus, basking in the warmth of his friendship. One of the great graces given us today is the practice of centering prayer, in which we can experience the presence of Jesus' spirit.

> *Centering prayer requires solitude and quiet. What are the difficulties in setting aside that kind of time?*
>
> *How can cultivating the art of attentive listening improve your prayer life? Or your daily life?*
>
> *When do you most feel the presence of Jesus?*

The family Jesus loved could properly be called a non-traditional one. But the labels most firmly attached are the ones given Martha and Mary. One doesn't have to look far these days to see the consequences of stereotyping persons. While some forms may be relatively innocuous, in its worst form, stereotypes can lead to grave injustices, even to war.

> *As a Catholic, have you ever felt the sting of prejudice? How did you react?*

In the words of a song, "You've got to be taught to hate and fear." Is that true? Can education change hearts for the better?

What is the role of the church in combating racism and other types of discrimination?

Prayer

Loving Martha and Mary,
Jesus graced you with his company,
For you understood the meaning of friendship.
Freely, frankly, you spoke to each other
As friends well know how.
What can you teach us
About listening to the Word,
With undivided attention,
To a Friend above all others?
Lord Jesus,
I, too, seek your friendship,
And the way is clear:
To put aside my busy-ness,
To give myself a quiet space
For you to enter into.
Then, centering my heart on you,
And you alone,
All my prayers are answered.

CHAPTER SIX

Mary of Magdala

Heartbroken, Mary and her friends approached the cave-like tomb carved out of rock, in a garden setting just outside of Jerusalem's city walls. The women were surprised to see that the heavy boulder sealing the entrance to the tomb had been rolled away. (They seem not to have planned in advance how to manage it themselves.)

The women came at first light of dawn that first day of the week, intent on anointing Jesus' body in a more reverential manner than was possible after his crucifixion and death late on Friday afternoon. A hitherto secret disciple, Joseph of Arimathea, had donated his own new garden tomb to the cause; and another secret follower, Nicodemus, had brought spices. Burial, of necessity, was hasty, for the Sabbath arrived at sunset and, according to Jewish law, nothing more could be done until it ended. The ensuing Sabbath had to be the longest one of their lives.

Now an even greater surprise awaits them. The women discover the tomb is empty! Adding to the mystery, a man dressed in white says something incredulous about Jesus having been raised from the dead. He further directs them to go and make known to the others what has happened. (Each of the four Gospels gives a slightly different version about the details, understandable when eyewitnesses are shaken by an event beyond their comprehension.)

Taking up the story from John's account: Mary of Magdala hurries to tell Peter and another disciple (presumably John) of the empty tomb, adding in anguish, "They have taken the Lord out of the tomb, and we do not know where they have laid him" (20:2). "They" might have been Roman soldiers or religious authorities, concerned that the tomb had the potential of becoming a place of pilgrimage for followers or Jesus, thus keeping alive the movement he started.

> "This Mary was the woman most prominent in the traveling band Jesus gathered in Galilee. She is mentioned by name fourteen times in the four Gospels, more than any other woman and more than most of the men in Jesus' inner circle."
> —Elliott Wright, *Holy Company: Christian Heroes and Heroines* (New York: Macmillan Publishing, 1980), p. 53.

The two apostles race back to the tomb with her, see only the burial cloths puzzlingly rolled up, and return to their hiding place. Mary, though, remains at the tomb weeping. Never has life seemed darker. Never has loss caused so much pain.

Suddenly, through a mist of tears, she becomes aware of a man standing near her. "Why are you weeping?" he asks. "Whom are you looking for?"

Thinking he must be the gardener, and would have some knowledge of what happened, she asks where the body was taken, ready on her part to do whatever necessary to recover it.

"Mary," he says in answer.

Disbelief for an instant is followed by the overwhelming realization that here at her side is the Master himself, transformed, yet recognizable by the way that only Jesus could speak her name. "Rabboni!" ("Teacher") she cries.

Suffused with joy, Mary thinks only of how to prolong the moment. But as was so often the case in the past, Jesus gives her a task to fulfill, and there is no time to waste. "But go to my brothers and say to them...," (John 20:17) he commissions her. She must do the work of an apostle—literally, "one sent."

Familiar with the men's place of refuge, she runs the half mile or so to deliver Jesus' message. Bursting into the room where they are gathered, she exclaims exultantly, "I have seen the Lord!" and goes on to tell of her experience and what Jesus wants them to know. But they refuse to believe her. "An old wives' tale," the men scoff. It would take the appearance of Jesus himself to convince them. In light of patriarchal thinking, their reaction was predictable. A woman's witness did not legally count. Yet each Gospel attests that women are the first to see the risen Christ, providing the witness necessary to the central tenet of the Christian faith: Jesus' Resurrection. Preeminent among these women is Mary of Magdala.

> "Another proof that women could be intimate disciples of Jesus is found in chap. 20 [John's Gospel].... It is clear that John has no hesitation in placing a woman in the same category of relationship to Jesus as the Twelve who are included in the 'his own' in 13:1."
> —Raymond E. Brown, s.s., *The Community of the Beloved Disciple* (New York: Paulist Press, 1979), p. 192.

Early in the Galilean ministry, she had become a part of it. By the time Luke tells of female disciples who belong to Jesus' company, she is seen as their leader.

> Soon afterwards he went on through cities and villages, proclaiming and bringing the good news of the kingdom of God. The twelve were with him, as well as some women who had

been cured of evil spirits and infirmities: Mary,
called Magdalene, from whom seven demons
had gone out, and Joanna, the wife of Herod's
steward Chuza, and Susanna, and many others,
who provided for them out of their resources
(Luke 8:1–3).

"The twelve were with him, as well as some women" makes
clear that the latter, too, accompany Jesus. The "many others"
suggests a sizeable band. The surest evidence of Mary's leadership shows in the placement of her name—always first on the
list in any enumeration of women disciples. Altogether, Mary's
name appears fourteen times in Gospel passages.

Among the women who are referred to by name in the
above passage, Susanna's is left without further identification,
either by town of origin or relationship to a male. It has been pro-
posed that she was still so well-known when the Gospels were
being written that additional explanation was unnecessary,
though it could as easily have been an oversight on Luke's part.

"Magdalene" is just another way of saying that Mary comes
from the town of Magdala, a prosperous one on the west coast
of the Sea of Galilee, situated between Tiberias (to the south)
and Capernaum (to the north). Though Magdala is mentioned
in the Gospels only in connection with Mary, and Jesus is never
reported to have visited there, it may well have been among the
"many towns and villages" where he preached and healed.

Magdala was of particular importance in first-century
Galilee because of its fish-processing center, which provided
one of the province's chief exports. After the process of pre-
serving fish had been perfected, the local economy received a
big boost. (Magdala's Greek name, Tarichaeae, is translated
"town of salt-fish.") Barrels of the commodity were shipped not
only around the country, but also abroad, as far away as Rome.
In Jerusalem, demand for the product was especially great during festivals. Galilean fishermen could always count on a ready
market for their catch.

How Mary acquired the wealth Luke attributes to her can only be guessed at. She may have operated a business in Magdala. It is conceivable that she then became acquainted with Peter and Andrew, James and John, during their fishing days. Another possibility is that she benefitted from a family inheritance. In any case, Mary enjoyed an independent status and would be free to engage in business if she chose, so long as a male guardian handled her legal matters.

At some point, Mary fell ill. The "seven demons" of which Jesus cured her must be understood in first-century Jewish terms, indicating a health problem of severity that baffled doctors. It has been conjectured that she may have suffered from either epilepsy or a nervous disorder, or perhaps a deep depression. Luke does not disclose where the miraculous cure took place—whether during healings on the Plain of Gennesaret, in the synagogue at Magdala or elsewhere in Galilee. Wherever or however it occurred, once restored to health, Mary committed her life and fortune to the furthering of Jesus' mission.

It is Mary who took the lead in unifying women of diverse social and economic status: fishermen's wives and mothers, a representative of court society and the "many others" of various backgrounds. To accomplish this, she must have been not only an effective organizer, but also regarded as deserving of their respect. A certain maturity would go along with that.

Aside from the women's practical everyday help, their financial assistance would have meant a great deal, since the Twelve had abandoned their occupations. All but John were thought to be married, and their families assuredly could use support. If any men provided material aid, none receives mention; though one of the Twelve, Judas Iscariot, "kept the purse."

In Matthew and Mark, at the scene of crucifixion, we belatedly hear of the women's contributions to Jesus' ministry dating back to Galilean days, though only in summary form. Matthew, for instance, observes that "Many women were also there, looking on from a distance; they had followed Jesus from Galilee and had provided for him. Among them were Mary Magdalene, and Mary the mother of James and Joseph, and the mother of the sons of Zebedee" (27:55–56). Mark says much the same, adding that "there were many other women who had come up with him to Jerusalem" (15:41).

Mary keeps her band together through the devastating hours of Jesus' crucifixion, when he was forsaken by almost all who had once flocked to his side, and during the darkness of the Sabbath, when all hope appeared lost. She rallied them on Easter morning to go to the tomb and pay their last respects. There was no one else to take charge.

After that first Easter, it remains for tradition and early Christian literature to fill in the blanks in the rest of Mary's story.

Afterword

According to tradition in the Eastern Orthodox Church, Mary of Magdala accompanied the Apostle John and Jesus' mother to Ephesus, in Asia Minor, where they spent the rest of their lives.

In early Christianity, the remembrance of Mary of Magdala's leadership comes through in second-century writings such as the apocryphal gospels (not accepted as canon). One of these gospels, in fact, was named for her. She and Peter are portrayed as rivals, reflecting the controversy developing over the question of women's official place in the church, for a hierarchy was in the process of being instituted.

In a church dating to circa A.D. 232, the first known painting of Mary was discovered in 1931 by archaeologists excavating Dura-Europos, a town on Syria's eastern border. The mural shows Mary of Magdala with a group of women going to the tomb, carrying torches and bowls of ointment.

Early Church Fathers, in their writings, praised Mary for her discipleship, never once questioning her moral character. Hippolytus of Rome, in a commentary written around the end of the second century or beginning of the third, was the first to call her the "apostle to the apostles." It became a favorite title for her. Augustine of Hippo (A.D. 354–430), however, tempered his praise by explaining why she had remained at the empty tomb: "out of the weakness of her nature," depicting her as overly emotional.

In the meantime, some biblical commentators began speculating whether the Mary of Luke's chapter eight might also be the unnamed "sinful woman" in his preceding chapter. It took a sixth-century pope, Gregory the Great, to deliver a fatal blow to Mary's unsullied Gospel reputation. Gregory governed in a licentious age, and moral reform was his goal. Deciding that Mary's "seven demons" stood for the seven capital sins (a theology just then being developed), and the worst one was promiscuity, he used Mary of Magdala as the prime example of how even the worst sinner could reform. So powerful and long-lasting was Gregory's influence, that his judgment of Mary continued into the twentieth century. Only in recent decades have scripture scholars begun to redeem her Gospel reputation.

The Eastern Orthodox Church, incidentally, has never seen her in any light other than its honorary title for her: "Equal to the Apostles."

Faith-Sharing Topics

During her grave illness, Mary discovered what was meaningful in life, what truly mattered. When we are confronted with the fragility of our existence, the important things of life become abundantly clear.

> *Discuss your priorities. Does your day-to-day life reflect them?*
>
> *Are there changes you would like to make? How much effort and adjustment would that take?*
>
> *How do you think making these changes would change you as a person?*

When all hope seemed lost, and the darkness overwhelming, Mary kept vigil, waiting despite not understanding. When darkness casts a shadow over our own life, when the hours and days seem endlessly bleak, we seek the comfort of faith.

Can there ever be an answer to the "why" of suffering?

In painful times, who or what has helped you through them?

When have you been a shoulder to lean on for others? How did it make you feel?

Prayer

Devoted Mary,
You kept faith in the midst of darkness,
Hope in the midst of despair.
Most of all, you remained loyal to Jesus.
In the beginning, you counted on him.
Later, he could count on you.
No wonder he chose you
To proclaim his greatest message—
Christ is Risen!
Lord Jesus,
When I feel forsaken,
Help me to remember
That you are my hope.
When storms rage around me,
Let faith carry me through,
A faith that never wavers.
In you lies my joy,
In you I find salvation.

CHAPTER SEVEN

Mary of Jerusalem

Scarcely believing what had just happened, Peter stood in the Jerusalem street in the dead of night. With the miraculous help of an angel of the Lord, he had narrowly escaped martyrdom; for his trial was scheduled to be held in the morning, and the outcome had already been decided. There was no time to lose in seeking refuge. At any moment the alarm was sure to sound, and the king's men would be on the hunt for him, wondering how he managed to escape, for guards had been chained to him on either side.

Peter headed for the one certain safe house, a half mile or so southwest of the Antonia Fortress, site of his imprisonment. Acts describes it as "the house of Mary, the mother of John whose other name was Mark, where many had gathered and were praying" (12:12). In fact, they were praying for Peter's deliverance.

His friends had good reason to worry. Shortly before, another valued member of their community, James (Salome's and Zebedee's son) had been beheaded on orders of King Herod Agrippa I, grandson of Herod the Great.

Peter stayed at Mary's house just long enough to tell the assembled group what happened to bring about his miraculous escape, and ask them to relay the news to another leader of their movement, another James, "brother of the Lord." Where Peter went into hiding after that was never revealed. He may have gone back home to Galilee; or, more wisely, three hundred miles north to Antioch, well out of reach of the king. Peter could easily lose himself in that city of half a million. Besides, Mary of Jerusalem's nephew Barnabas would be there to welcome Peter and ensure his safety.

> "[Mary of Jerusalem] governs a household large enough to employ servants, and it is no small thing for her to open this residence to other believers. Such gatherings angered an empire that labeled the Jesus movement 'subversive,' making clandestine meetings necessary."
> —Rose Sallberg Kam, *Their Stories, Our Stories: Women of the Bible* (New York: Continuum, 1995), p. 253.

At an earlier time, Barnabas had been sent from Jerusalem to take charge of the congregation in Antioch, composed of Gentiles as well as Jews converted to belief in Jesus. (The term "Christian" originated in Antioch.) When King Agrippa died unexpectedly two years after Peter's imprisonment, Peter was free to return to their headquarters in Jerusalem. (After Agrippa's death, Rome reverted once more to direct rule of Palestine by a Roman governor.)

Members of the Jesus movement could breathe easier for the present, free now to concentrate on building up the community of believers. Mary of Jerusalem's house served as the gathering place for followers of "the Way," as the movement was popularly called. Mary apparently was a widow of some means. Her house was located in an upscale neighborhood, not far from the mansion of the high priest. She had put her home at the disposal of the disciples, and many think that her Upper Room was the scene of the Last Supper. It may be recalled that Jesus had dispatched Peter and John to attend to the details in reserving a furnished room spacious enough to accommodate their group, telling the two apostles they would know whom to contact by following a man carrying a water pitcher—a seemingly impossible assignment, considering the jam-packed streets of Jerusalem during Passover. Except that fetching water, regarded as a menial task, was left for females to do. Consequently, a man would stand out in the crowd. Some suggest that Mary's son, John Mark, carried out this assignment. It would indicate then that Mary was a disciple of Jesus long before her name is mentioned midway through the Acts of the Apostles.

Some important events in Acts took place in what is referred to as the "Upper Room." In the very first chapter, Peter speaks at a meeting of believers who "numbered about one hundred twenty persons . . ." (1:15). Archaeologists confirm that upstairs rooms in the holy city were often large enough to accommodate a crowd of 120.

Excavations disclose much about the lifestyle of the wealthy in first-century Jerusalem, whose society included prosperous landowners and merchants, royalty, Roman administrators and the aristocratic class of priestly families, some of whom were also landowners of large estates. They lived in the western sector, called the Upper City, which was divided from the eastern half by the Tyropoeon Valley (long since silted up). A bridge spanned the valley, giving residents easy access to the Temple. Standing at a slightly

> "Besides being the site of Jesus' Last Supper and the supposed site of Jesus' appearances to his disciples after his Resurrection, the Upper Room has been traditionally the place filled by the Holy Spirit at the time of the Jewish feast of Pentecost."
>
> —John J. Kilgallen, S.J., *A New Testament Guide to the Holy Land* (Chicago: Loyola University Press, 1987), p. 222.

higher elevation than the eastern ridge, the western hill caught the fresher breezes and also enjoyed more breathing space in terms of the layout. It contrasted sharply with the Lower City, situated to the south of the Temple. This section was home to the working poor, who lived in crowded conditions, amidst the noisy bazaars and smells of all kinds wafting through a maze of narrow lanes and stepped streets.

Mansions in the Upper City thus far uncovered have been compared to the first-century Roman villas of Pompeii. Among their features: tiled roofs and elaborate plumbing systems that provided for luxurious bathrooms. Interiors were richly decorated with frescoed walls and mosaic floors. It was common to have an upper room, often with an outside stairway, in order to accommodate large receptions or provide a meeting place.

If Mary's house were even half as elegant, it would have been a far cry from the typical fisherman's abode in Galilee— though not so unusual for the well-to-do women who formed part of Jesus' circle. What counted far more than the decor was the hospitality Mary extended in putting her home at the disposal of the disciples. It may have been here that the male disciples went into hiding after Jesus' arrest, and possibly where Jesus made several post-Resurrection appearances. Inside a room with the doors locked, says John.

Based on the weight of ancient tradition, along with what may be deduced from Acts, Mary's house from beginning days provided the setting for important events in the infant church, in addition to being a regular gathering place for prayer and the breaking of bread.

At first, members of "the Way" continued to attend both synagogue and Temple, for the final break with Judaism was yet to occur. But they also needed quarters of their own in which to meet privately. (An understanding of themselves as distinct from Judaism evolved in a slow and painful process. Other Jews thought of Jesus' followers then as just another sect of their faith, referring to them as Nazarenes.)

Jerusalem contained scores of synagogues, including a number for those Greek-speaking Jews from the Diaspora who had relocated to the holy city—Mary's nephew Barnabas among them. He originally came from the island of Cyprus, possibly to study as Paul had. Some suggest that Barnabas was one of the seventy unnamed disciples of Jesus (Luke 10:1). As Acts reports, Barnabas sold a farm he owned in Cyprus, turning over the proceeds to the community.

Mary's family contributed generously in service as well as funds. Her own role has been overshadowed by the events in her home, and by the activities of her better-known son and nephew. Both achieved prominence as missionaries, and to John Mark is attributed the Gospel bearing his name.

Mary, in fact, receives but a single mention in the New Testament, when Peter seeks refuge in her home after his escape from prison. He knew where to find the support he needed at a critical time. It had been a dozen years since the Ascension of Jesus, attesting to Mary's long-term faithfulness as a disciple.

In its first chapter, having recounted the Ascension, Acts tells of the men and women returning afterward to the Upper Room where they had been staying. "All these [names of the apostles] were constantly devoting themselves to prayer, together with certain women, including Mary the mother of Jesus, as well as his brothers" (1:14). This is the first intimation that Jesus' kinsmen, once opposed to his public life, had come to believe in him. (As no other household has been identified as hosting significant events in the formative years of Christianity, it is reasonable to assume that the Upper Room must have continued to be the one belonging to Mary.)

Acts goes on to say: "When the day of Pentecost had come, they were all together in one place" (2:1). They were awaiting the promised Holy Spirit to guide them. And as we know, their hopes were fulfilled.

That event resulted in many conversions, but also drew increasing attention from the authorities, who began targeting leaders of the movement. Sporadic arrests followed, though imprisonment was generally of short duration. The more that tensions between Jews and their Roman masters increased, the more were Jews expected to adhere to orthodox Judaism as a sign of national unity. In these circumstances, private quarters for the disciples' gatherings became doubly important.

Regardless of the risk to herself (for the high priest resided nearby), Mary kept her house open to the comings and goings of the "church" that met in her upper room. She would have been busy with the logistics involved: scheduling times for meetings and prayer services along with instruction of new members; making arrangements for sleeping quarters when needed; shopping for food and preparing meals. In other words, providing the stability necessary for a movement in order to set down roots. One can see the pattern being laid for the early Christians' basic institution, the house church.

In her behind-the-scenes work, Mary would be privy to the decision-making when major questions had to be resolved. The chief issues of the day were whether Gentiles should be admitted to the movement and, if so, whether male Gentile converts must first submit to circumcision.

Some Pharisees and priests had joined "the Way," bringing with them a more conservative viewpoint. This was reflected in heated discussions at the first Church Council in Jerusalem, circa A.D. 49–50. The site of that council is not mentioned in Acts. Perhaps at Mary's house?

Afterword

The founding of Christianity in Egypt is attributed to Mary's son John Mark. Tradition says he was martyred there. Barnabas met a similar fate in Salamis, Cyprus. It is reasonable to assume that Mary devoted the rest of her days to the welfare of the church. That her house served long past her lifetime as a center of Christianity is testified to by historical remembrances and traditions. Though other places of assembly would have been required in Jerusalem as the membership grew, her house became known as "the mother of all the Churches." Had it been possible to preserve the original building, Mary's home might well rival that of Peter's and his wife's as the oldest Christian sanctuary still in existence.

As it is, pilgrims today still venerate the historic shrine believed to occupy the site of Mary's house. The continued presence of a Christian community in Jerusalem since New Testament times made it possible for knowledge of holy places in the city to be handed on from generation to generation. The original house was believed destroyed during a persecution by the Emperor Diocletian in A.D. 303, but the site was remembered. A few decades later, when Queen Helena came to the Holy Land to erect shrines with Gospel associations, she had the cherished memories to aid her.

Later in the fourth century, an even larger church was built on the traditional spot and given the name "The Upper Church of the Apostles." Subsequent to that, a succession of buildings were to occupy the site and the present one, dating to medieval times, is now known as the *cenacle* (from the Latin word for "dining room"), or room of the supper. An appropriate designation in memory of Mary's generosity in providing a home for the first Christians.

Faith-Sharing Topics

Mary models all of the unsung in the first generation of Christians, serving the practical needs without which there could be no church. In every congregation, there are men and women who work tirelessly behind the scenes for the well-being of its members.

Some of the unsung members in our faith community are...

We acknowledge their contributions by...

What percentage of parishioners would you guess are active members?

What would it take to motivate others to volunteer?

We know this Mary best because of her house. Through her magnificent spirit, it became the center of Christianity in Jerusalem. In our churches, we look for ways to bring about an atmosphere of togetherness and show the kind of hospitality that makes people feel they truly belong.

How can a sense of family be created in a large congregation? Does it automatically happen in a smaller parish?

What are the most complimentary words you can say about your parish?

Which area of parish life could use improvement? How can you help make that improvement?

Prayer

Gracious Mary,
You gave without thought of recompense,
Without thought of honor.
Even now, not many know your name,
Or how essential you were to the Way of the Lord.
Lacking "Mary's house,"
Where else would the disciples have gathered
For prayer, for refuge,
While awaiting the Holy Spirit?
Holy Spirit,
We'd be lost without you
And your treasury of gifts,
Of graces galore,
Available for the asking.
What shall I ask for today?
A welcoming heart, a generous spirit,
And when they are used up,
I'll ask again.

CHAPTER EIGHT

Tabitha of Joppa

Within a few years of Christianity's first Pentecost in Jerusalem, the Way of the Lord had spread to the coastal plain. For centuries the town of Joppa on the Mediterranean coast had served as chief port for Jerusalem, which lay thirty-five miles inland. In that capacity, Joppa's harbor had the honor of being the point of entry for cedars that King Solomon had ordered to be shipped from Lebanon to build the first Temple. Joppa served the same purpose when cedars were needed once more, this time to rebuild the Temple after its destruction during a war with the Babylonians. Scripture not only tells about these events, but also gives the legendary account of Jonah's attempt to avoid going on an evangelizing mission to the Gentiles of Nineveh, a mission ordained by God. Instead, Jonah boards a ship at Joppa, intending to head in the opposite direction.

The biblical references recall an important past and times of prosperity—days long since gone. The downhill slide of Joppa had begun during the reign of Herod the Great, when he decided to construct a new, much grander harbor thirty miles up the coast. While the plan fit in with Herod's fondness for building on a monumental scale, some say he had an ulterior motive: retribution for the stiff resistance put up by the people of Joppa when Herod came marching through the country on his way to claiming the kingship granted him by Rome.

Upon completion (shortly before Jesus' birth), the magnificent harbor for the newly created city of Caesarea Maritima ("on the sea") attracted much of the business that formerly benefited Joppa. Another drawing card: the splendid amenities of Caesarea, typical of any Greco-Roman city.

Even more to the point in practical terms, a tremendous breakwater to ensure the safety of ships at anchor was constructed. Considered a miracle of engineering, the breakwater extended two hundred feet out into the Great Sea, as the Mediterranean was called.

Much of the straight-running coastline of Palestine was barren of natural harbors. Until the advent of Caesarea, Joppa had been the only viable one lying between the Egyptian border ninety miles south of it, and Acco, seventy miles north.

> "Acts probably reflects historical experience in stressing that women were involved in the Christian missionary movement at every stage of its expansion. Tabitha of Jaffa represents the first stage of expansion..."
> —Elisabeth Schüssler Fiorenza, *In Memory of Her: A Feminist Theological Reconstruction of Christian Origins* (New York: Crossroad, 1984), p. 167.

But the Joppa harbor had its drawbacks. For one thing, though the huge rocks surrounding it formed a naturally sheltered basin, a stiff enough wind could also drive boats up against the rocks. Joppa was subject to a "black north wind," as first-century historian Josephus described it. The wind was capable of pushing masses of sand from the sea bottom in toward land, silting up the harbor, and making it too shallow for the larger ships that had come to dominate the maritime trade.

Although some smaller merchant ships still sailed into the harbor, commerce in general lost out to the greater advantages offered by Caesarea. The chief users now were local fishermen who, for the most part, eked out an existence for themselves and their families. Between the wind and the rocks, wooden fishing boats broke up all too often, leaving widows and fatherless children with little means of support.

Stepping in to provide relief was a woman belonging to the town's Christian community. She had taken Jesus' teachings about loving service to heart. As Acts describes her: "Now in Joppa there was a disciple whose name was Tabitha, which in Greek is Dorcas. She was devoted to good works and acts of charity" (9:36). Both the Aramaic Tabitha and its Greek counterpart, Dorcas, signify "gazelle," a Jewish symbol for grace and beauty. And beautiful she was to the people who worked with her, as well as to the recipients of her works of compassion.

Tabitha may have been a widow; in any event, hardly penniless, for she had her own home, one with an upstairs room—the usual indication of someone with more than average means. And she had the leisure to engage in charitable acts.

> "Tabitha became an early convert to Christianity. . . . After her conversion, Tabitha worked to become like Christ in every aspect of life. Like Peter, James, John, and the others, Scripture calls Tabitha not just a believer, but a disciple."
> —Julie-Allyson Ieron, *Names of Women of the Bible* (Chicago: Moody Press, 1998), p. 172.

It was a disastrous blow to all concerned when Tabitha succumbed to an illness. Acts relates that Peter happened to be in Lydda, ten miles away. Two men from Joppa brought him the sorrowful news that a valued member of their community had died. Peter was asked to come back with them at once, since burials customarily took place within twenty-four hours.

Peter arrived to find the deceased lying in an upstairs room, with the body prepared for burial. Mourners had gathered around to grieve over their loss. At sight of Peter, they tearfully showed him the numerous garments Tabitha had made, awaiting distribution to the needy. They also spoke of her many charitable deeds.

Peter tells them to go downstairs while he prays over the body. Alone, he kneels to ask the Lord's help. Then, reminiscent of words he had heard Jesus speak, Peter commands, "Tabitha, get up" (9:40).

Miraculously, she opens her eyes. When Peter takes her by the hand, she is able to stand, and they go downstairs—an appearance greeted with great rejoicing. News of Tabitha's restoration to life spreads like wildfire through the town, drawing many more to faith in Jesus.

Touching as the conclusion is, the story bears closer examination beyond the wonder of the healing miracle. To begin with, when Peter presents a glowing Tabitha to the assembled company, a clear distinction is made between the "saints" and the "widows" who are present. In New Testament times, saints (from the Greek for "holy ones") designated Christian believers. As for widows, there were two classes understood by the early church: widows in the ordinary sense; and women who belonged to a group engaged in works of a pastoral nature. The widows gathered in Tabitha's home appear very much to be on familiar ground; not as recipients of aid, but knowledgeable about all of her good works. When Peter first arrived, they had displayed the many items of clothing produced while Tabitha was still with them. Clothing made with them, not for them—a cooperative effort. Tabitha's is the earliest known evidence of women organized in a ministry of their own devising, and may well have served as the prototype for what eventually became formalized into an order in the church.

The first formalized ministry for men occurred in Acts 6, when seven were appointed to do table service, to see that those widows (in the ordinary sense) in the faith community being neglected would receive enough to eat. This task freed the apostles to concentrate on their evangelizing mission. A ritual laying-on of hands, later regarded as ordination, accompanied the appointment. The origin of the office of deacon is traced to this event. As it turned out, the seven did not confine themselves to table service. Best-known among their number was Stephen, martyred in the mid-30s, about the same time as Tabitha's restoration.

The women's group in Joppa appears without preamble, apparently banding together voluntarily, under the direction of Tabitha. From the very start, charity played a prominent part in Christianity. (It may be noted that when men care for poor widows, it is referred to as "ministry." When women do the same, they are seen as doing "good works.") Later in the New Testament, in the First Letter of Timothy, an ecclesiastical order of widows is recognized. Dating for this epistle ranges from the latter part of Paul's career to near the end of the first century. Rules by this time are being imposed on women:

> Let a widow be put on the list if she is not less than sixty years old and has been married only once; she must be well attested for her good works, as one who has brought up children, shown hospitality, washed the saints' feet, helped the afflicted, and devoted herself to doing good in every way. (5:9–10)

It was thought then that younger women were not emotionally equipped for the commitment demanded, and were encouraged instead to remarry after being widowed.

Afterword

Though in practice, women of fifty could enroll, the purpose of the age requirement cited in the First Letter of Timothy was to fit in with the legal system, particularly the marriage laws of Rome.

The order of widows initiated by Tabitha played a significant role in the first centuries of the church, with its members engaging in intercessory prayer as well as pastoral work. Second-century Apostolic Fathers such as Ignatius of Antioch and Polycarp wrote about its existence in their time.

In A.D. 313, when Christianity received state approval, many more conversions resulted. Because older widows were not always able to meet the strenuous demands of expanded ministerial duties, their order eventually merged with the office of deaconess.

Joppa (modern Jaffa), today a suburb of Tel Aviv, has several churches named in honor of Peter: one, a Franciscan; another, Russian Orthodox. In the courtyard of the Russian church, visitors are shown the Tomb of Tabitha. Her memory further survives in organizations that bear the Greek form of her name, Dorcas. For example, in 1980 in the Netherlands, Dorcas Aid International was founded to provide social development and relief aid. Partnering with Christian organizations and churches, it funds projects in more than twenty countries, involving thousands of volunteers worldwide.

Faith-Sharing Topics

Affected by the sight of suffering in her town, Tabitha felt compelled to do something about it. Genuine compassion is more than a "feeling sorry for" the individual suffering. It moves one to take action.

> *Someone once said that the world can't be mended; it can only be loved. How do you respond to that statement?*

> *In hearing that a friend, neighbor or fellow parishioner is ill, you are inclined to...*

What do the spiritual and corporal works of mercy mean to you?

Tabitha's dedication inspired other women to join her in doing good works. Thus was born the order of widows involved in prayer and service. In our own time, Mother Teresa began her ministry by helping one person. Soon a former student decided to join her—a modest start to a worldwide ministry.

Identify some of the major humanitarian needs in your community. Do you feel they are being sufficiently addressed?

How involved is your parish in outreach ministry? Locally? Nationally? Globally?

As an individual, how can you make a difference?

Prayer

Tenderhearted Tabitha
With utter devotion,
You sought out the suffering poor,
Tending to their needs.
Praying for others was a part of your ministry,
Prayers that weave invisible ties of love.
People loved you, and no wonder,
For how Christlike you were.
Holy Spirit,
Inspire in us the desire to bring comfort,
To aid those in want,
Whether neighbors next door or in far-off places.
Make us channels of compassion,
Praying for good and doing good.
In our works of mercy,
We help to build
God's kingdom on earth.

CHAPTER NINE

Lydia of Philippi

The Apostle Paul first set foot on European soil circa A.D. 50, in response to a dream or vision. It occurred, fortuitously, at Troas, chief port for departures from Asia Minor to the continent of Europe. In the dream, a Macedonian man beckoned Paul to come to his territory; though, as it turned out, a woman in Macedonia would become his first convert there. A province of the Roman Empire, Macedonia extended from northern Greece westward across the Balkan Peninsula to the Adriatic coast.

The 156-mile crossing from Troas to Neapolis, nearest entry point to the continent, took only two days due to favorable winds. To avoid the perils of navigating in darkness, the ship had dropped anchor overnight at a midway point, the island of Samothrace. Accompanying Paul were Silas, Timothy and Luke. A Gentile convert, Luke appears to have joined the missionary team at Troas.

After they disembarked at Neapolis, the men had another ten miles inland to go before reaching Philippi—about a three hours' walk. The city was one of the most important in

Macedonia, owing to its location on the Via Egnatia. This major commercial and military highway, second most important in the empire, cut across the Balkan Peninsula to link the East (the Aegean region) with the West (the Adriatic). In his evangelization efforts, Paul purposely selected urban centers positioned along busy highways as a key to spreading the faith. The practice had worked effectively ever since missionary work expanded beyond Palestine.

> "For merchants such as Lydia the dealer in purple goods, who was from Thyatira (Asia Minor) but met Paul in Philippi (Macedonia) (Acts 16:14), travel was an occupational necessity —and hazard."
>
> —Wayne A. Meeks, *The First Urban Christians: The Social World of the Apostle Paul* (New Haven, Conn.: Yale University Press, 1983), p. 17.

Once the men reached their destination, Paul looked for the local synagogue in order to give fellow Jews a chance to hear his message of Good News. In almost every major city in the empire, a viable Jewish quarter could be found. But in that respect, Philippi proved disappointing. So modest was the Jewish community, it apparently lacked the requisite number of ten male heads of households to form a synagogue.

Undaunted, on the Sabbath Paul and his companions walked south of the city gate along the riverbank, searching for a likely place where Jews might gather for prayer, even without a synagogue in the usual sense. (Water was necessary for the ablutions integral to worship.) They met with success, finding a group composed of women engaged in prayer, including some Gentiles known as "God-fearers." The term referred to individuals who were attracted to the Jewish faith and attended services, but had yet to make a final commitment.

On that historic day, Paul gained his first converts on European soil: among them, a Gentile woman named Lydia. A seeker of spiritual truth not found in the prevailing Hellenistic culture of the empire, Lydia eagerly embraced Paul's teachings. In fact, she, along with members of her household, were baptized on the spot—the rite being facilitated by their presence near a water source.

Lydia originally came from Thyatira, a city in the western part of Asia Minor. She was a cloth merchant, a dealer in purple goods used for the kind of garments worn by royalty and other persons of wealth. Hers was consequently a prosperous trade, giving her the independence to head a household of her own. A merchant's household, unlike the more traditional kind, would be composed not only of family members and servants or slaves, but also of hired laborers and sometimes business clients. As a result, it represented an economic as well as a social unit.

To understand why Lydia's entire household would follow her lead and also convert: according to the practice of the time, its members could count on their head for security; and they, in turn, gave their loyalty. For that reason, it was not at all unusual for everyone in a household to belong to the same religious cult.

> "Upon becoming a Christian, Lydia opened her home to the missionaries, persuading them to accept her hospitality. Luke no doubt sees her as a major force in laying the foundations for the church in Philippi."
>
> —Evelyn and Frank Stagg, *Woman in the World of Jesus* (Philadelphia: Westminster Press, 1978), p. 230.

There were numerous cults to choose from, wherever one lived in the empire. Most of these religions were transplants from the East. They professed devotion to various gods and goddesses, depending upon the place where the cult originated, and were often referred to as "mystery religions" because of their secret rituals.

Cults were acceptable to Rome as long as they did not detract from allegiance to the empire or adversely affect public order. The primary concern of the official state religion was the welfare of the empire. A privileged group known as the Vestal Virgins bore responsibility for a ritual thought to ensure that welfare, in which they tended the sacred fires in the temple of the goddess Vesta. Only six females served in the position at any one time (and that with a thirty-year commitment). Women otherwise played little part in state religion.

Cults flourished because they filled a spiritual hunger, answering the need to feel that life holds meaning, and providing that sense of belonging inherent in a close-knit religious community.

Women were especially drawn to cults of goddesses, which gave them a better chance of acting in an official capacity, whether in hosting cult worship in their own home, or in some cases participating in ceremonies even as a priestess. Philippi was known to have several strong female figures among the deities with sanctuaries in the city.

Since it originated in the Near East, the Jewish faith came under the umbrella of mystery cults, but was distinguished by its insistence on belief in only one God, and by ethical principles that set a much higher standard.

One wonders if, in preaching to the small assembly on the riverbank, Paul found it advantageous to mention that in Christianity women enjoyed opportunities for ministry denied them in Jewish religion, in which females always remained secondary to males. To God-fearers in general, he could offer the monotheism and morality they sought, yet without the ritual requirements of Jewish law: circumcision for men, and for women, the restrictive measures surrounding menstruation and childbirth. (In a century or two, some in the Christian hierarchy would begin raising objections to "unclean" females attending worship services.)

Lydia may have become a God-fearer while still in her native city of Thyatira, known to have a Jewish community. Thyatira was noted for its trade in purple goods. Artisans there had developed a method for making a purple vegetable dye from the madder root—an alternative to the more costly dye derived from the rare murex shellfish in Phoenician waters. Philippi was reported to have a source for the madder root, which could have been one of the reasons Lydia decided to relocate her business, at least for the time being. Mobility was common to merchants and artisans seeking to expand their business. Though relatively small in size for an urban center, Philippi's boundaries extended well into the surrounding countryside, with its towns, villages and farms all needing the administrative and commercial services of the city.

An idea of what ancient Philippi looked like came to light in the early part of the twentieth century, when French archaeologists excavating the site found the remains of what they called "a remarkably beautiful Greco-Roman city." It claimed all the desirable features of other, much larger, cities in the empire: a forum, agora (marketplace), theatre, public baths, gymnasium and temples and shrines honoring an assortment of divinities. In addition, the Via Egnatia bisected the center of the city—a boon, of course, to merchants and traders. Philippi's status as a Roman colony governed by Roman law would prove helpful to Paul later, when he ran into trouble, which happened to him rather often.

In the meantime, Lydia persuaded Paul and his companions to lodge in her home for the duration of their stay. (Women in Macedonia enjoyed a greater freedom of action than was found in many other provinces of the empire.)

As a result of her hospitality, Lydia's home became the first house church established by Paul on the European continent. The Christian congregation that grew from this simple beginning was one that Paul would always hold in the deepest affection. In a New Testament letter to the Philippians a few years later, he tells of his love for them and calls them "my joy and crown."

During his stay in the city, Paul exorcised a possessed slave girl, an action that enraged her owners. The girl had been a moneymaker for them, using her gift of divination to tell fortunes. Because Silas was with Paul at the time, he too was accused, flogged and jailed. It was a short-lived imprisonment, however. At a hearing the next morning, the magistrate learned that Paul held Roman citizenship; and as such, should not have been jailed without a trial. (Being a native of Tarsus, Paul fell heir to Roman citizenship granted that city.) The magistrate requested, though, that Paul leave the area for the sake of maintaining the peace. But first Paul returned to Lydia's house to settle affairs before departing with Silas and Timothy. Luke stayed behind, whether to ensure a solid base for Lydia's fledgling house church, or possibly at Luke's own request. The physician may have wanted more time to check out Philippi's famous medical school. He eventually rejoined Paul.

In the years that followed, Paul made several happy return visits to the Philippians, writing letters between visits to congratulate them on their spiritual progress and to express gratitude for their generosity to him. Though Paul counted on Christian hospitality wherever his travels took him, he prided himself on the fact that he earned his own living. But in a break from his usual policy of not accepting monetary gifts, he gladly accepted help from the Philippians. Such was the nature of their relationship with Paul.

Afterword

House churches like Lydia's were essential in laying a firm foundation upon which the greater church would be built. Until Christianity received official sanction from the Emperor Constantine in the fourth century and intermittent persecutions ended, congregations met in private homes to avoid public scrutiny.

Lydia may eventually have returned to Thyatira, for her name does not appear in the New Testament after the events of Paul's initial stay in Philippi. In the Book of Revelation written three or four decades later, Thyatira is one of seven cities addressed as a center of Christianity. Might she have been instrumental in establishing the church there?

In his own letter to the Philippians (circa A.D. 110), Bishop Polycarp (believed to have known the Apostle John) writes that he rejoices "because the firm root of your faith, famous from the earliest times, still abides and bears fruit for out Lord Jesus Christ" (quoted from *Early Christian Fathers,* edited by Cyril C. Richardson [New York: Macmillan Company, 1995], p. 131).

Faith-Sharing Topics

Despite living in a pagan environment, with idol worship of all kinds, Lydia did not succumb to their seductive trappings, but persevered in seeking God. In our own time, idols are more subtle, but they can be just as powerful in detracting from a God-oriented life.

> *Can you identify some of the current idols?*
>
> *What is their impact on the young? How do they affect you?*
>
> *What can be done to negate the influence of false idols?*

In her pilgrim journey to find faith, Lydia experienced that transforming moment when she reached her goal. In our inner journey of faith—a sometimes bumpy road—we seek a deeper spirituality.

> *When have you felt the transforming power of a parish mission or a retreat away from home?*
>
> *Some books or authors you would like to recommend as an aid to a more enhanced spiritual life are ...*
>
> *What is the most important thing to remember on your journey of faith?*

Prayer

Persevering Lydia,
Ever searching, refusing to settle for less,
You reached your destination,
That wondrous moment of awe,
At last to have found God.
Rewarded with faith,
You looked now for service.
How else to express
Praise and thanksgiving!
Holy Spirit,
Be with me on my journey,
My unseen Companion.
Be my guide and strength.
If I stumble,
Set me aright.
The road is marked with milestones.
For those long passed and those to come,
Glory be to God.

Chapter Ten

Prisca, Coworker of Paul

In the spring of A.D. 52, Prisca, her husband Aquila, and their traveling companion, the Apostle Paul, set sail from Corinth to begin the next phase of their ministry. The voyage would take them 250 miles directly east, across the Aegean Sea to Ephesus, fourth largest city in the Roman Empire.

The three had become acquainted eighteen months before, when Paul arrived from Athens in a state of discouragement. His efforts at evangelization in the intellectual center of Greece netted him only a few conversions. Since he earned his living by leather-working, Paul had sought out that quarter in the marketplace of Corinth. There he met Prisca and Aquila, who invited him to work alongside them and share their living quarters.

Paul soon learned that the couple were not natives of Corinth, but had been among the Jews expelled from Rome in A.D. 49, on orders of Emperor Claudius. According to the Roman historian Suetonius, rioting in the city's Jewish quarter had erupted over a religious dispute "at the instigation of Chrestus." (Rome thought that Christians were just another sect of Judaism.)

Because of threats on its borders at the time, Rome—with national security always an issue—could ill afford disturbances in the very heart of the empire. Jews formed a sizeable minority in the capital city, with estimates ranging between twenty and fifty thousand. Perhaps not all were expelled, but for expedience, only the more visible leaders in the dispute. Judging from their subsequent activities, Prisca and Aquila likely fell into the leadership category.

> "...a number of reputable scholars have presented strong cases in favor of Priscilla being the author of the canonical Letter to the Hebrews."
>
> —Leonard Swidler, *Biblical Affirmations of Woman* (Philadelphia: Westminster Press, 1979), p. 317.

While Acts says Aquila originally came from Pontus on the Black Sea, tradition goes further, describing him as a freedman who made his way to Rome, where he married Prisca, she from a high-born family. This was not an uncommon situation. Freedmen, by the way, were former slaves who won their release either by working for it, or purchasing it outright. Depending on prior education, a slave might labor in menial jobs or serve in clerical positions. Prisca's own educational background becomes apparent later, when she gives instruction to a famous orator. (In Paul's letters, he calls her Prisca, while in Acts, Luke uses the diminutive form, Priscilla.)

In Corinth, Prisca and Aquila carry on their commercial business, which proves a useful base for making converts. They also sponsor a church that meets in their house, probably a carryover from their life in Rome. Meanwhile, Paul focuses his attention on trying to convince local synagogue members that Jesus fulfilled their expectations of a Messiah. Therefore, they should accept the gospel message. Paul had some success, including conversion of the synagogue's leader. But he also had opponents, and they brought a charge against him before the Roman proconsul in Corinth. Though the proconsul dismissed the charge, Paul felt the time was right to move on to new fields. Having grown to depend on Prisca's and Aquila's help, he asks them to accompany him to Ephesus.

But their departure, first of all, must be timed to fit in with sailing season, which went from late spring to early fall. Navigation depended on the position of the sun and stars, and winter skies obscured them. Winter storms also made sea journeys hazardous. The three also had to wait for a vessel with space available, since cargo received preference.

With the arrival of spring, they were soon on their way. Because most ships had sleeping accommodations only for the captain, passengers, like the crew, lived on deck, sometimes under tent-like shelters. They brought their own food, which could be cooked in the galley. Water for everyone was stored in large wooden tanks in the hold of the ship.

The time spent at sea—ten days or more—could be used advantageously: reflecting on what they had learned from their experiences in Corinth and making plans for the work ahead. As with any new venture, excitement mingled with a measure of apprehension.

> "According to Acts the beginnings of the church in Ephesus are associated with Prisca and Aquila (Acts 18:18–19). The frequent mention of this couple...indicates their importance in the early years of the church."
> —Frederick J. Cwiekowski, s.s., *The Beginnings of the Church* (New York: Paulist Press, 1988), p. 111.

The journey nears its end when the ship leaves the Aegean to sail into a narrow, three-mile-long channel of the Cayster River, leading to the harbor at Ephesus. As they dock, Prisca and the others can look up to see the broad avenue running in a direct line from the harbor, through the heart of the city, and terminating at a 24,000-seat amphitheatre that curves into the slope of Mount Pion.

Out of sight (though probably not out of mind) is the Ephesians' greatest attraction, the famous Temple of Artemis, a mile and a half northeast of the city. The Artemision, as it is called, had earned the distinction of being named one of the Seven Wonders of the World because of its magnificence. But sightseeing does not rate high now on the list of priorities for the three missionaries. Getting settled takes precedence. A place must be found in which to set up shop. Equally important, obtaining lodgings large enough to accommodate both living quarters and space for the Christian community they expect to organize. (Archaeologists say that anywhere from twenty to fifty persons might convene in a typical house church. Homes with a courtyard could accommodate fairly large gatherings.)

There were undoubtedly converts already, both Jews and Gentiles, in Ephesus. They could be found in virtually every urban center in the empire. What the city lacked so far was leadership with the resources to sponsor a house church. Paul leaves the details in the capable hands of Prisca and Aquila in order to concentrate on converting members of the local synagogue. When, after a few months, the response continues to be disappointing, Paul leaves Ephesus to travel first to Jerusalem, and afterward to visit several parts of Asia Minor where small congregations had previously been founded. Then he would return.

For the next three years, Prisca and Aquila worked tirelessly at building up a Christian community, supporting it with income derived from their leather-making shop. Overseeing a house church entailed a variety of responsibilities. Foremost, preparation must be made for the at least weekly celebration of the Lord's Supper. (The earliest extant testimony for the Eucharistic words of consecration comes in a letter Paul wrote to the Corinthians after his move to Ephesus. See 1 Corinthians 11:23–25.) In addition to Eucharist, the worship service included prayers, singing of hymns and Scripture readings.

"Scripture" then consisted of texts from the Hebrew Bible; for although Jesus' words and deeds were recalled orally, they had yet to be committed to writing. That would occur a decade or two later.

Christian communities kept in touch with each other across the empire through the exchange of letters that were read aloud to the assembly. Visiting missionaries also brought news, as did Christian merchants passing through. The hospitality extended to these visitors ranked as one of the indispensable practices of a house church.

During the week, members engaged in ministry to others: visiting the sick and imprisoned, giving alms to the needy and, for those qualified, instructing new members about the Way of the Lord.

It was during Paul's absence that a brilliant Scripture scholar, Apollos of Alexandria, arrived in Ephesus. When Prisca and her husband heard him address the synagogue (Jewish Christians were still attending its services), they realized he had an incorrect understanding of the faith he professed in Christ, despite his great learning. Inviting Apollos to their home, Prisca and Aquila enlightened him. He accepted with good grace being taught by a woman as well as a man. Setting Apollos straight proved a benefit to the church at large, as he continued his preaching around countries of the Mediterranean basin.

Subsequently Paul returned, and again tried to make conversions at the synagogue. Again his efforts bore little fruit. For the next two years he rented a lecture hall and devoted himself to preaching there. Paul proved the most successful in whipping up opposition to certain practices beloved by the Ephesians. He was able to persuade some of the Christians to prove that faith had changed their lives by holding a public burning of scrolls dedicated to the magical arts. Ephesus was a center for magical arts, and the scrolls were of considerable value.

What happened next provoked an even greater outcry. Paul targeted false idols; namely, replicas of the temple and of the goddess Artemis. These medals were crafted by silversmiths, whose livelihood depended upon selling such objects as votive offerings or souvenirs to devotees of Artemis. The pilgrim trade, in fact, was the city's major economy.

Acts describes the scene in which a silversmith named Demetrius rallies his colleagues in the guild of craftsmen to take action. They collar two men identified as associates of Paul, and drag them down the main avenue of the city toward the amphitheatre. The scuffling and shouting—"Great is Artemis of the Ephesians!"—attracts attention; and in short order a huge crowd collects.

Paul wants to speak to the crowd, but wiser heads prevail, and he is smuggled out of the vicinity. The chief city official addresses the people instead, arguing convincingly that a serious disturbance would invite a crackdown by Roman authorities, causing everyone to suffer as a result.

Not long after the near riot, important news arrives from Rome. In October of the year 54, Emperor Claudius had been poisoned by his wife, and her son (Claudius' stepson) took the throne. The seventeen-year-old Nero rescinded the ban against exiled Jewish Christians, enabling Prisca and Aquila to return home. There they will host another church in their house.

In a letter Paul writes to the Romans a few years later, it is likely the incident of the silversmiths that he refers to in saying: "Greet Prisca and Aquila, who work with me in Christ Jesus, and who risked their necks for my life" (Romans 16:3–4).

Afterword

The missionary labors of Prisca and Aquila extended over a wide area of the empire, in three of its key cities: Rome, Ephesus and Corinth. (Troubles in Corinth did not arise until after their departure.) It is not known whether the couple were martyred during Nero's persecution about ten years after their return, though seventh-century guides for pilgrims to

Rome refer to a burial place in the registry of martyrs' graves. The Church of St. Prisca on Aventine Hill in Rome is said to stand over the site of her house church. She was highly esteemed by early Church Fathers. Incidentally, whenever Prisca and Aquila are mentioned in the New Testament, Prisca's name most often comes first, implying her prominence.

Ephesus became one of the chief centers of Christianity in the early centuries. According to tradition, John's Gospel was written here (circa A.D. 90); and as remarked previously, Jesus' mother may have spent her last years in Ephesus. In A.D. 431 the third Church Council met in a church dedicated to Mary. (Devotion to Mary by then had replaced that given to Artemis.) A sixth-century basilica stands over the traditional site of John's grave.

Faith-Sharing Topics

In the early church, it was common for Christians like Prisca and Aquila to assume roles of an ecclesiastical nature. A male priesthood and hierarchy were subsequent developments. Although lay Catholics had long been involved in matters of charity and social justice, it was not until after Vatican II that laypersons were invited to engage in ministries once the prerogative solely of clergy and religious.

> *If there were to be no shortage of religious vocations in the future, do you think that lay liturgical ministries would disappear? If not, why not?*

> *In what way does participation of laity in the liturgy invigorate your faith community? Laypersons formally trained for full-time service to the church are becoming more visible. How can we support their special vocation?*

In founding house churches, Prisca and Aquila made utmost use of the opportunities that presented themselves in their workplace, bringing Christ to others. Similar opportunities await us in office, factory, shop or wherever else we spend our workday, serving God in everything we do.

How can Christian values be integrated into the way business is conducted?

When disagreements arise among employees, when temperaments clash, are you ready to risk acting as a peacemaker? What are ways of going about it?

How else can you put faith into practice— evangelizing by example—while on the job?

Prayer

Blessed Prisca,
Such an evangelist you were,
Traveling the empire East and West.
Exiled from home,
You turned an unhappy event into opportunity,
Bringing the gospel to new audiences
In cities ripe for conversion.
Through missionaries like you,
Thus did the church grow and prosper.
Holy Spirit,
Kindle in me a burning desire to spread Good News
Wherever I find myself,
Whatever the circumstances of my life.
I pray for opportunity,
Believing your gift of fortitude
Will carry me forward.
I give thanks in advance
For your holy gift.

CHAPTER ELEVEN

Phoebe, Deacon of Cenchreae

Mission accomplished! With the precious document in hand, Phoebe reaches Aventine Hill in southwestern Rome, home of Prisca and her husband Aquila. Phoebe is about to experience a joyous reunion with old friends, eager to hear about her long journey and ask about the latest happenings in Corinth and her own congregation in Cenchreae.

Once the initial exchanges are over, Phoebe explains why she is here. Paul, she tells them, had come to Corinth for a return visit that winter (A.D. 57–58) at the same time that she was making plans to go to Rome on business.

He asked her to deliver this letter, to be shared among the house churches in Rome. (There was no mail service for the public.) Naturally she brought it first to Prisca and Aquila, since they had worked so closely with Paul in the past. In fact, they are the first ones to be addressed in what came to be known as the scriptural "Letter to the Romans."

The others who are addressed represent the leadership of Rome's various house churches. No single church is dominant. The relationship they have with each other appears to be amicable. (Information about the founding of Christianity in Rome is lacking.) From the wording of the greetings, it seems that Paul has had contact with some of the leadership in the past, while they were in Paul's part of the world.

It is his fervent hope that they will provide the support he needs for an anticipated mission to Spain, once he takes care of business in Jerusalem. Meanwhile, Paul entrusts Phoebe with his message, which includes a comprehensive explanation of all that he believes about the Christian faith.

For the benefit of church leaders who might not be personally acquainted with Phoebe, he makes clear that she is much more than a letter carrier:

> I commend to you our sister Phoebe, a deacon of the church at Cenchreae, so that you may welcome her in the Lord as is fitting for the saints, and help her in whatever she may require from you, for she has been a benefactor of many and of myself as well. (Romans 16:1–2)

Paul puts a surprising amount of information into that one sentence. The reader learns that Phoebe heads a congregation in her own right in the harbor town of Cenchreae. She is given several titles related to her activities and, as noted, has also been of help to Paul. (The New Testament mentions Cenchreae one other time, as the place where Paul takes a vow before embarking for Ephesus with Prisca and Aquila.)

Cenchreae served as one of Corinth's two seaports, a situation owed to Corinth's location: on the isthmus connecting mainland Greece with the Peloponnesus, the peninsula that formed the southern half of Greece. Both geography and navigational needs made the isthmus pivotal to commerce between East and West, and that brought much prosperity to the area. It also brought a cosmopolitan mix of human traffic: merchants, immigrants in search of new opportunities, sailors and government officials. For Corinth was capital of the Roman province of Achaia (the lower half of Greece). The two harbor towns serving it came under Corinth's jurisdiction. Population of the isthmus has been estimated at 100,000 or more.

Phoebe's town, six miles east of the city of Corinth, faced onto the Saronic Gulf, an inlet of the Aegean Sea. Ships arrived from Egypt, Syria and Asia Minor. On the opposite, western side of the isthmus lay the other port, Lechaion, handling vessels from Spain, Italy and other points west. Both ports benefited from the fact that navigating around Cape Malea, the southernmost tip of the peninsula two hundred miles distant, could be extremely hazardous. A Greek saying rightly advised: "Let him who sails around Malea forget his home and make his will." To safeguard valuable cargo, ship captains generally opted for the safety promised in using the isthmus route.

A tramway had been built at the narrowest part of this neck of land, more than three miles across. Ships could be unloaded at one port and cargo hauled to the opposite one, then reloaded onto another vessel. When small enough, the boat itself could be transported across land on wooden rollers, along a paved road designed for the purpose.

A short distance north of Cenchreae were the grounds for the Isthmian Games, held in alternating years with the Olympic Games at Delphi, though on a smaller scale. This meant an influx of spectators, athletes and touring entertainers—among them, fortune-tellers. Facilities for the games included a stadium, theatre, temple and sacred grove. The festival began with a sacrifice to Poseidon (Neptune to the Romans), Lord of the Sea, followed by a variety of competitions in athletics and music.

Despite the paganism attached to the games, and the moral laxity generally associated with a port serving a host of nationalities and cultures, the congregation in Cenchreae seems to have escaped any adverse effects. To Phoebe's credit, nothing is heard about dissension or a faltering in faith among the membership, either in Paul's letters or elsewhere—and he never hesitated to admonish where corrections were due.

Phoebe directed her congregation independently of him. Her house church must have been firmly established by the time of Paul's arrival in Corinth, circa A.D. 50, for there is no suggestion that he had any part in its founding. And the preceding year, upon their arrival, Prisca and Aquila had been occupied in setting up their own house church.

It was Paul who counted on support from Phoebe, according to the reference in his letter to the Romans. The help she gave may have been through her influential position in the community. In New Testament Greek, he describes her as *prostatis*. Translations of the title vary, depending upon the bible consulted: benefactor, helper, good friend. But there was a definite understanding of the word in the secular world. The meaning encompassed the idea of ruler, leader, protector. That is, someone with the necessary authority to represent persons or groups in matters to do with government or legal issues. (Paul had his share of those.)

> "Paul's letters were written on papyrus ... sheets were attached end to end to make scrolls—Paul's Letter to the Romans would have needed a scroll some 13 feet long. It was probably rolled and sealed."
> —Kaari Ward, ed., *Jesus and His Times* (Pleasantville, N.Y.: Reader's Digest, 1992), p. 290.

His other title for Phoebe, *diakonon* (deacon), has often been translated as "deaconess," but that office, *diakonissa*, did not come into existence until several centuries later, when women's role in the church had diminished. After that occurred, a deaconess attended women only: assisting, for instance, at baptism, in which immersion was the norm. In Phoebe's time, "deacon" was a fluid term, functions differing from place to place.

When Paul writes to the Romans in A.D. 56–57, we see Phoebe still ministering in Cenchreae. Hers is a long-term commitment. It was probably in the early spring of A.D. 57 that she departed for Rome, combining her own business with that of delivering Paul's letter. Though going by sea was generally the faster way to travel, a safe voyage early in the spring could not be guaranteed. Many more people in the first century preferred an overland route. It has been said that, until the advent of the steamship in the latter part of the nineteenth century, the public had never traveled more than in the first century. Roman roads and a military presence facilitated that movement as did the widespread use of Greek, the international language understood almost everywhere. Moreover, going from one province to another in the empire required no passport.

Individuals were free to join a caravan if they wished. In any case, they would go in company of some sort. One suspects that a woman of Phoebe's class would travel with a servant or two, and perhaps business associates or some members of her congregation.

Two major highways built by the Romans connected the eastern part of the European continent with Rome. Phoebe and her companions would first make their way north to reach the Via Egnatia, which cut across northern Greece and the rest of the Balkan Peninsula, terminating at the Adriatic coast. Owing to demand, ferries operated frequently, some as passenger-only ships. Crossing the Adriatic Sea took two days. From the Italian port of Brindisium, the Via Appia ran 350 miles across countryside, veering north to the city of Rome.

> "Her [Phoebe's] mention at the head of a long list of names—associated with the male form of the title for 'deacon'—may indicate that hers was a special role and that Paul was introducing her to the Romans as his trusted associate, preparing the way for his mission to Spain."
>
> —Richard A. Horsley and Neil Asher Silberman, *The Message and the Kingdom: How Jesus and Paul Ignited a Revolution and Transformed the Ancient World* (Minneapolis: Fortress Press, 2002), p. 190.

On her journey, Phoebe would find posting stations at intervals of twenty to thirty miles on main roads, more often than that where there were towns along the way. These stations offered a range of services. Arrangements could be made to hire transport, for example. Options included light carriages pulled by mules or horses, ox wagons or donkeys that carried goods or people. Soldiers and government couriers changed horses at posting stations, and a surprising number of travelers walked.

For government officials and military personnel, there were rooms and bathing facilities of an acceptable standard. Public inns, however, were often little more than brothels, to say nothing of squalid conditions. But thanks to the policy of establishing faith communities in urban areas along well-traveled trade routes, Christians on a mission like Phoebe's would be able to count on Christian hospitality at least some of the time. A network of business contacts could offer a welcome at other times.

Phoebe's story in the New Testament ends after the delivery of Paul's letter. Once she had met the leaders of other house churches, and her business affairs in Rome were concluded, she would have returned home to her duties in Cenchreae.

Afterword

Perhaps Phoebe was still administering her church in the year A.D. 66, when Emperor Nero arrived on a concert tour. (He fancied himself an accomplished musician.) While there, Nero turned the first shovel of dirt for a canal at the isthmus. Six thousand Jews, prisoners from the war that had begun with Rome, were commandeered from Palestine to do the actual construction. But due to his superstitious nature, Nero changed his mind, believing the entire peninsula might slide into the sea if the work proceeded.

The Letter to the Romans was the subject of a commentary by the theologian Origen, writing in the 200s. In it, he makes reference to Phoebe, observing: "This text teaches with the authority of the Apostle that even women are instituted deacons in the Church." (Quoted in Roger Gryson, *The Ministry of Women in the Early Church* [Collegeville, Minn: Liturgical Press, 1978], p. 31.)

In the first generation of Christianity, a woman sponsoring a house church may well have presided over the Eucharistic meal and preached to the congregation that met in her home. In small gatherings in private quarters, well out of public view, there would not be the problem of talk generated about women assuming liturgical roles in worship services.

The extent to which women engaged in ministerial duties did not appear to become an issue of serious debate until the second century, when the movement of the Spirit began giving over to a human imperative for regulations thought necessary for the maintenance of order and orthodoxy. With growth, church offices became formalized, and a male hierarchy took shape. Fitting in more closely with the ways of the surrounding secular culture assured greater acceptance of Christianity—and possibly its survival, since Roman authorities always kept a suspicious eye on religions of foreign origin. Perhaps understandable for that period of history, the visible role of women diminished. In the ensuing centuries, they would find creative ways to serve Christianity and the church.

Phoebe is best known today, not for her contributions as patron, minister, evangelist and all-round benefactor but, rather, for the debate engendered by the title given her in Paul's letter: deacon. A better understanding of the impact of culture upon religion might well illuminate the debate.

Faith-Sharing Topics

In ministering to her house church, Phoebe welcomed a cosmopolitan mix of nationalities, ethnic groups and economic classes, even slaves—all of them treated as equals. The changing face of the Catholic Church in America brings with it the rich gifts of diversity, but also the problem of how to promote inclusivity.

> *In your view, which is preferable: multicultural parishes or separate ethnic communities?*

> *In a multicultural parish, how can the needs of different ethnic groups be balanced? Separate liturgies? Shared liturgies?*

> *What is the individual parishioner's obligation in creating a receptive atmosphere and respecting the devotional practices of other cultures?*

Phoebe served her congregation in multiple roles, as did other women in New Testament times. But rules to restrict their ministries lay on the horizon. One of the liveliest topics in the twenty-first-century church revolves around the question or extent of women's participation in church offices.

> *How do you think the pain and anger on the part of some over the issue of women's ecclesial roles, including leadership positions, affects the life and mission of the church?*

> *What is the greatest obstacle to an open discussion on the possibility of women's ordination either as deacon or priest?*

> *Can you see any value in further research and reflection on women's participation in the early church?*

Prayer

Gifted Phoebe,
Your name means "bright light."
How brightly you shone the light of Christ
Upon all in your care.
In mission at home and mission abroad,
You never tired of service,
Garnering words of praise.
For all that you were, all that you did,
We salute you.
Holy Spirit,
May your spirit ennoble ours,
As we open wide the doors
To discover that, in community
Diversity is not adversity.
Not when we worship together,
Bear one another's sorrows, and
Share one another's joys.
To this, we shout a resounding "Amen."